# Bible Brain Builders, Volume 5

# Other Bible Brain Builders

*Bible Brain Builders, Volume 1*

*Bible Brain Builders, Volume 2*

*Bible Brain Builders, Volume 3*

*Bible Brain Builders, Volume 4*

# Bible Brain Builders

## Volume 5

THOMAS NELSON
*Since 1798*

NASHVILLE   DALLAS   MEXICO CITY   RIO DE JANEIRO

Published in Nashville, Tennessee, by Thomas Nelson. Thomas Nelson is a registered trademark of Thomas Nelson, Inc.

Book design and composition by Graphic World, Inc.

Original puzzles and mazes created by W. B. Freeman.

Thomas Nelson, Inc., titles may be purchased in bulk for educational, business, fund-raising, or sales promotional use. For information, please e-mail SpecialMarkets@ThomasNelson.com.

The material in this book originally was published in other forms in *Nelson's Super Book of Bible Word Games, Book 1*, © 1992, *Nelson's Super Book of Bible Word Games, Book 2*, © 1993, *Nelson's Super Book of Bible Word Games, Book 3*, © 1993, *Incredible Mazes, Book 1*, © 1993, *Incredible Mazes, Book 2*, © 1994 by Thomas Nelson Publishers, Inc., all rights reserved.

Unless otherwise noted, Scripture quotations are taken from THE NEW KING JAMES VERSION. © 1982 by Thomas Nelson, Inc. Used by permission. All rights reserved.

Verses marked KJV are taken from the HOLY BIBLE: KING JAMES VERSION

Verses marked NIV are taken from the HOLY BIBLE: NEW INTERNATIONAL VERSION®. © 1973, 1978, 1984 by International Bible Society. Used by permission of Zondervan Publishing House. All rights reserved.

ISBN: 978-1-4185-4936-7

*Printed in Mexico*

14 13 12 11 QG 1 2 3 4 5 6

# THE THANKFUL ONE

*It*'s hard to imagine forgetting to thank someone who literally hands you back your life. But this is exactly what happened to Jesus one day. Upon entering a certain village, ten men afflicted with leprosy cried out to Jesus for mercy. When these men realized they were healed, only one of them returned to thank Jesus and give glory to God.

Only one man's path will lead to Jesus in the corner. Begin at each man until you find the thankful one.

2

Sometimes doubts, worries, and cares overtake us. What's the solution? "Seek first the kingdom of God" (Matthew 6:33).

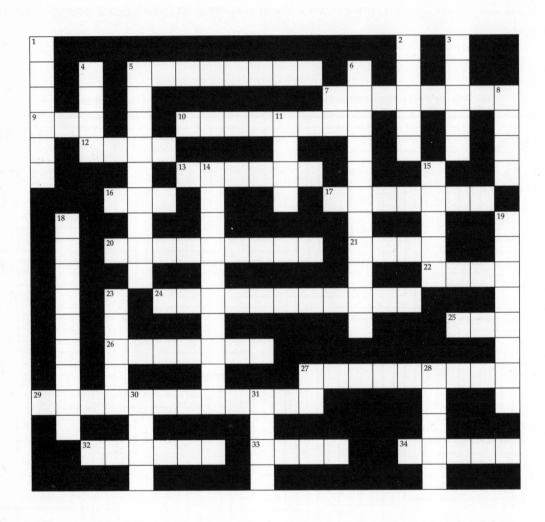

## Across

5 They worry about food, drink, and clothing (Matthew 6:31–32)

7 Don't have "fights" over doubtful things like dietary laws (Romans 14:1)

9 She doubted God's word about the Tree of Life (Genesis 3:4–6, 20)

10 They'll come in the last days and question the Second Coming (2 Peter 3:3–4)

12 Can a risen _____ man persuade those who doubted Moses and the prophets? (Luke 16:31)

13 Cast your "problem" on the Lord (Psalm 55:22)

16 With no doubt, you can wither a _____ tree (Matthew 21:19–21)

17 "Be _____ for nothing" (Philippians 4:6)

20 "I want you to be without care," Paul said, speaking of staying "single" (1 Corinthians 7:32)

21 Let's _____ about Jesus

22 Don't worry; God is on our _____

24 Your heart can be "encumbered" by the cares of this life (2 words) (Luke 21:34)

25 This king of Judah, perhaps doubting God's support, allied with the king of Syria (2 Chronicles 16:7)

26 Gideon still had doubts, even after squeezing this much water from his fleece (Judges 6:38)

27 "Are You the 'Expected' ?" asked John's disciples, displaying some doubt (2 words) (Luke 7:20)

29 Does unbelief make the "loyalty" of God ineffective? (Romans 3:3)

32 She was needlessly "worried and troubled about many things," said Jesus (Luke 10:41)

33 Thomas, also known as the _____ , doubted Jesus' resurrection (John 20:24–25)

34 Paul wanted men to pray without "ire" and doubting (1 Timothy 2:8)

## Down

1 His clan was the weakest in Manasseh—how could he defeat the Midianites? (Judges 6:11–17)

2 When this creature fastened itself onto Paul's hand, the Maltese said, "No doubt this man is a murderer" (Acts 28:3–4)

3 His doubt got him wet (Matthew 14:29–31)

4 The Israelites wouldn't "listen to" Moses; they doubted a divine rescue (Exodus 6:9)

5 Paul had doubts about them; they seemed to prefer the law (Galatians 3:1–2; 4:20–21)

6 Have compassion on some making a "differentiation" (Jude 22)

7 Doctor (abbr.)

8 Doubting scribes and Pharisees needed a "guidepost" from Jesus (Matthew 12:38)

11 Another word for worry (Psalm 37:7)

14 Worldly cares make us "unproductive" (Matthew 13:22)

15 Jesus did fewer of these in His hometown because of unbelief (Matthew 13:58)

18 He was made mute for doubting Gabriel's word (Luke 1:18–20)

19 Doubt nothing, the Spirit told Peter. Go see Cornelius in this city (Acts 10:1, 20)

23 Can worry add one _____ to your stature? (Matthew 6:27)

27 First two initials of Narnia author

28 By believing, Martha would see the "magnificence" of God (John 11:40)

30 Don't fret; it only causes "damage" (Psalm 37:8)

31 "But he who doubts is condemned if he 'feeds'" (Romans 14:23)

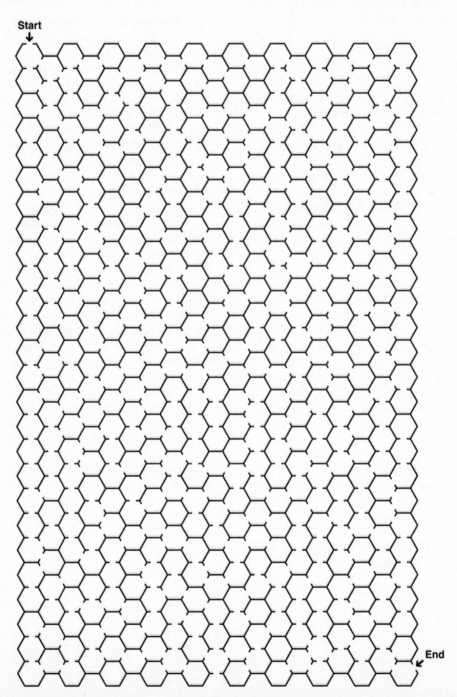

*P*roverbs 16:24 tells us, "Pleasant words are like a honeycomb, sweetness to the soul and health to the bones." See how quickly you can make your way through the honeycomb maze below!

Start

End

*P*rovide the names of the wives of the Bible men below to complete the acrostic, which gives us the name of the most cherished "wife" of all time and eternity.

1. Boaz and _____          (Ruth 4:13)
2. Jehoiada and _____      (2 Chronicles 22:11)
3. Heber and _____         (Judges 4:21)
4. Zacharias and _____     (Luke 1:5)
5. Er and _____            (Genesis 38:6)
6. Elimelech and _____     (Ruth 1:2)
7. Isaac and _____         (Genesis 24:67)
8. Abraham and _____       (Genesis 20:2)
9. Nabal and _____         (1 Samuel 25:3)
10. Lapidoth and _____     (Judges 4:4)
11. Moses and _____        (Exodus 2:21; 18:2)
12. Amram and _____        (Exodus 6:20)
13. Joseph and _____       (Genesis 41:45)

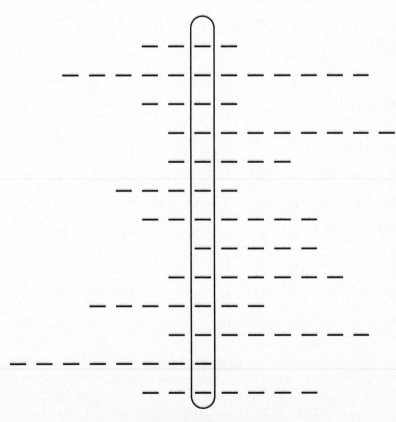

(Revelation 21:9)

*T*he Bible describes the human heart in many different ways. Find twenty of these "states of heart" in the box of letters below. (See how many you can find before you consult the Scripture Pool.)

```
S  E  A  B  R  O  A  E  D  E  C  E  I  T  F  U  L
L  O  H  C  W  F  R  O  S  N  C  D  O  U  P  R  U
V  W  E  S  O  S  F  D  I  W  U  O  N  N  L  F  F
E  I  A  E  R  N  U  E  L  P  R  O  U  D  I  U  R
M  L  V  R  R  S  F  C  L  C  E  W  S  E  W  S  A
E  L  B  U  O  D  E  U  K  S  I  Y  R  R  E  M  E
R  I  C  R  S  I  E  X  S  F  T  S  E  S  F  I  F
R  N  H  U  D  E  C  E  E  I  U  S  O  T  R  O  B
G  G  I  A  R  P  N  D  P  L  O  E  S  A  A  N  R
N  N  S  E  R  D  N  C  O  L  K  N  O  N  E  S  O
F  U  I  F  A  F  U  L  V  C  M  E  R  D  F  S  K
N  I  O  L  D  E  C  E  I  W  I  G  P  I  A  S  C
O  S  G  L  B  R  S  N  E  K  O  R  B  N  T  E  H
C  O  I  L  R  M  R  E  W  G  Y  A  I  G  S  N  I
U  W  N  I  Y  R  E  I  M  V  N  L  D  N  R  T  N
O  S  G  N  I  H  C  R  A  E  S  V  L  D  E  N  V
R  G  C  O  S  K  R  E  T  O  S  E  R  N  E  I  Y
R  W  I  U  E  P  H  K  C  I  W  S  E  U  R  A  L
O  S  N  D  O  U  D  D  E  C  E  I  S  U  F  F  L
```

### Scripture Pool
EXODUS 35:5   LEVITICUS 26:36   DEUTERONOMY 28:28, 47, 65
JUDGES 5:15, 16   1 KINGS 3:9; 4:29   PSALMS 12:2; 34:18; 64:6; 101:5
PROVERBS 14:30; 15:13; 17:20; 25:20; 26:23   ISAIAH 35:4

*U*se the numbers under the letters to complete the passage below.

```
B   L   E   S   S   E   D       I   S       T   H   E       M   A   N       W   H   O       W   A   L   K   S
1   2   3   4   5   6   7       8   9       10  11  12      13  14  15      16  17  18      19  20  21  22  23

    N   O   T       I   N       T   H   E       C   O   U   N   S   E   L       O   F       T   H   E
    24  25  26      27  28      29  30  31      32  33  34  35  36  37  38      39  40      41  42  43

    U   N   G   O   D   L   Y,      N   O   R       S   T   A   N   D   S       I   N       T   H   E
    44  45  46  47  48  49  50      51  52  53      54  55  56  57  58  59      60  61      62  63  64

    P   A   T   H       O   F       S   I   N   N   E   R   S,      N   O   R       S   I   T   S       I   N
    65  66  67  68      69  70      71  72  73  74  75  76  77      78  79  80      81  82  83  84      85  86

    T   H   E       S   E   A   T       O   F       T   H   E       S   C   O   R   N   F   U   L;
    87  88  89      90  91  92  93      94  95      96  97  98      99  100 101 102 103 104 105 106

B   U   T       H   I   S       D   E   L   I   G   H   T       I   S       I   N       T   H   E       L   A   W
107 108 109     110 111 112     113 114 115 116 117 118 119     120 121     122 123     124 125 126     127 128 129

    O   F       T   H   E       L   O   R   D,      A   N   D       I   N       H   I   S       L   A   W
    130 131     132 133 134     135 136 137 138     139 140 141     142 143     144 145 146     147 148 149

    H   E       M   E   D   I   T   A   T   E   S       D   A   Y       A   N   D       N   I   G   H   T.
    150 151     152 153 154 155 156 157 158 159 160     161 162 163     164 165 166     167 168 169 170 171
```

```
___  ___      ___  ___  ___  ___  ___      ___  ___      ___  ___  ___  ___       ___
118  12       36   88  139   21  127      107   31      147  168   22   91       162

___  ___  ___  ___      ___  ___  ___  ___  ___  ___  ___      ___  ___      ___  ___  ___
83  102  151   6        65    2   56   74  156  114  161         1   50       124   11  134

___  ___  V   ___  ___  ___      ___  ___      ___  ___  ___  ___  ___,     ___  ___  ___  ___
76  142      159   80  121      130   40       19  164   93   64  137      171  110   66   55

___  ___  ___  ___  ___  ___      ___  ___  ___  ___  ___      ___  ___  ___      ___  ___  ___  ___  ___
107  53  155   24   46   99       70   94   80  158   42      122   62   71       95   53  105   82   29

___  ___      ___  ___  ___      ___  ___  ___  ___  ___  ___,     ___  ___  ___  ___  ___
27  167      145  119    4        90    3  157   59   18   35      149  150  101  112   89

___  ___  ___  ___      ___  ___  ___  ___      ___  ___  ___  ___  ___      ___  ___  ___
106  37   92  104      128   38    9   25        5  133   20  127   49        15   69   26

___  ___  ___  ___  ___  ___;     ___  ___  ___      ___  ___  ___  ___       V  ___  ___
129   8   96  125  126  102        14  165   48       16   97   14   10   98      43  137

___  ___      ___  ___  ___  ___      ___  ___  ___  ___  ___      ___  ___  ___  ___  ___  ___  ___.
30  151        7   79  153  160      121   17   92  115  135       65  102   33  146   65   12   53
```

(Psalm 1:1–3)

The noblest of women is described in Proverbs 31. The words that complete this passage are also the words you need for the crossword grid. See how far you can get before consulting your Bible.

Who can find a _____ wife? For her
<sub>18 Across</sub>

_____ is far above _____ . The _____
<sub>17 Across</sub>     <sub>16 Down</sub>     <sub>24 Across</sub>

of her _____ safely _____ her; so
<sub>45 Down</sub>     <sub>15 Down</sub>

_____ will have no lack of gain. She
<sub>19 Across</sub>

does _____ _____ and not _____ all
<sub>45 Across</sub> <sub>56 Down</sub>     <sub>5 Across</sub>

the days of her life. She _____ _____
<sub>26 Down</sub> <sub>44 Across</sub>

and _____ , and willingly works with
<sub>9 Down</sub>

her hands. She is like the merchant

_____ , she brings her _____ from
<sub>35 Across</sub>     <sub>48 Down</sub>

_____ . She also rises while it is _____
<sub>8 Across</sub>     <sub>58 Down</sub>

_____ , and _____ food for her house-
<sub>55 Across</sub>   <sub>11 Across</sub>

hold, and a portion for her _____ . She
<sub>27 Down</sub>

considers a field and _____ it; from her
<sub>53 Across</sub>

_____ she plants a _____ . She _____
<sub>39 Down</sub>     <sub>29 Across</sub>     <sub>37 Across</sub>

herself with strength, and _____ her
<sub>32 Down</sub>

_____ . She _____ that her _____ is
<sub>13 Across</sub>   <sub>1 Down</sub>     <sub>6 Down</sub>

good, and her _____ does not _____
<sub>43 Down</sub>     <sub>37 Down</sub>

_____ _____ night. She stretches out
<sub>62 Down</sub> <sub>57 Across</sub>

her hands to the _____ , and her _____
<sub>46 Across</sub>     <sub>59 Across</sub>

holds the _____ . She extends her
<sub>30 Down</sub>

_____ to the poor, _____ , she reaches
<sub>21 Across</sub>     <sub>23 Down</sub>

out her hands _____ the _____ .
<sub>36 Down</sub>   <sub>2 Down</sub>

She is not afraid of _____ for her
<sub>12 Down</sub>

household, for all her household is

clothed with scarlet. She makes _____
<sub>36 Across</sub>

for herself; her _____ is fine linen and
<sub>42 Across</sub>

_____ . Her husband _____ known
<sub>1 Across</sub>     <sub>63 Across</sub>

_____ the_____ , when he _____
<sub>7 Across</sub> <sub>14 Across</sub>     <sub>4 Down</sub>

_____ the elders of the land. She _____
<sub>47 Down</sub>     <sub>31 Across</sub>

linen _____ and _____ them, and
<sub>22 Down</sub>     <sub>54 Down</sub>

_____ _____ for the _____ . Strength
<sub>50 Across</sub> <sub>25 Across</sub>     <sub>20 Down</sub>

and _____ are her clothing; she shall
<sub>52 Across</sub>

rejoice in time _____ come. She _____
<sub>34 Across</sub>     <sub>49 Down</sub>

her mouth with _____ , and on her
<sub>28 Across</sub>

_____ is the _____ of kindness. _____
<sub>10 Down</sub>     <sub>61 Across</sub>     <sub>33 Across</sub>

watches over the ways of her house-

hold, and does not _____ the _____ of
<sub>51 Down</sub>     <sub>41 Across</sub>

_____ness. _____ children rise _____
<sub>40 Down</sub>   <sub>59 Down</sub>     <sub>38 Across</sub>

and call her blessed; her husband also,

and _____ praises her: "Many _____
<sub>65 Across</sub>     <sub>64 Across</sub>

have _____ well, but you excel them
<sub>60 Down</sub>

_____ ."
<sub>3 Down</sub>

# LOADING THE BOAT

Noah was a "just man" who was righteous before God. For that reason, Noah and his family were saved from destruction when God decided to destroy all other life on dry land by a flood. God told Noah to build a large craft into which he was to gather his family and two of "every living thing of all flesh" so that the earth might be replenished when the flood waters receded (Genesis 6:19).

It is interesting to speculate whether or not this gathering of animals included fish and other sea creatures since they could have survived the flood on their own.

Help Noah with the complicated task of gathering *all* the animals into the ark. Do not cross over any of your paths.

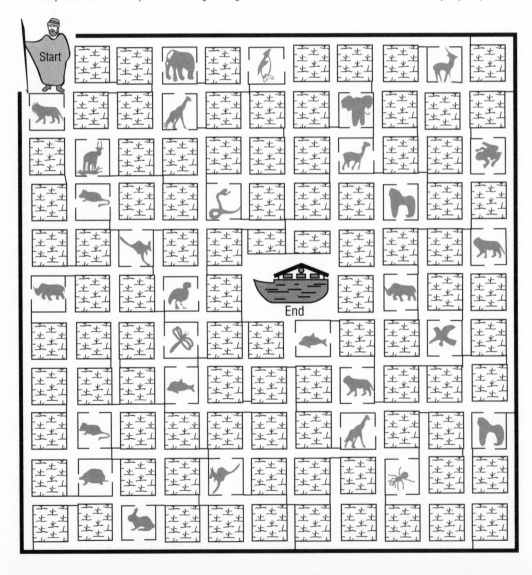

*S*olve the cryptogram below to reveal five specific commands that the apostle Paul gave to the Corinthians.

*Clue:* MESSIAH *is* 15 2 20 20 3 1 11

—— —— —— —— —— ,  —— —— —— —— ——   —— —— —— ——   —— ——
23  1  21  7  11    20  21  1  16  8    9  1  20  21    3  16

—— —— ——   —— —— —— —— —— ,   —— ——   —— —— —— —— —— ,
21  11  2    9  1  3  21  11    6  2    6  19  1  22  2

—— ——   —— —— —— —— —— —— .   —— —— ——   —— —— ——
6  2    20  21  19  4  16  10    14  2  21    1  14  14

—— —— —— ——   —— —— ——   —— ——   —— ——   —— —— —— ——
21  11  1  21    25  4  5    8  4    6  2    8  4  16  2

—— —— —— ——   —— —— —— —— .
23  3  21  11    14  4  22  2

# THE GOOD SHEPHERD

*T*he symbolism of the Good Shepherd is found in both the Old and New Testaments. In Psalm 23, David asserts, "The LORD is my shepherd" (v.1). Jesus, too, used the example of the shepherd. In a parable, He told of the shepherd with one hundred sheep and he posed a question: If the shepherd loses one sheep, will he not leave the other ninety-nine to go and search for the lost one? Jesus' care for us, His sheep, is so profound, that He is in constant search of the lost sheep among us.

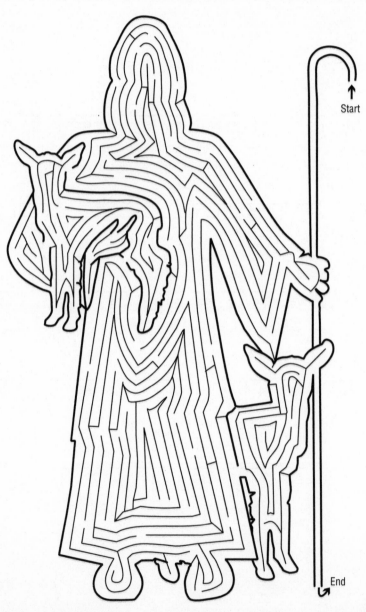

Start

End

One of the most frequently repeated commands in the Bible is that to "Rejoice!" Complete these verses about rejoicing to discover a special theme they share in common.

1 "Let the _____ of those rejoice who seek the LORD" (1 Chronicles 16:10)

2 "You shall rejoice in your _____" (Deuteronomy 16:14)

3 "God had made them rejoice with great _____ " (Nehemiah 12:43)

4 "Break forth in _____ , rejoice, and sing praises" (Psalm 98:4)

5 "You shall rejoice in every _____ _____ which the LORD your God has given to you and your house" (2 words) (Deuteronomy 26:11)

6 "Then shall the virgin rejoice in the _____" (Jeremiah 31:13)

7 "Let the _____ rejoice, and all that is in it" (1 Chronicles 16:32)

8 "You shall rejoice in all to which you have put your _____" (Deuteronomy 12:7)

9 "Rejoice, O _____ , with His people; for He will avenge the blood of His servants, and render vengeance to His adversaries; He will provide atonement for His land and His people" (Deuteronomy 32:43)

10 "Let the _____ rejoice, and let the earth be glad" (Psalm 96:11)

11 "In Your _____ they rejoice all day long" (Psalm 89:16)

12 "My _____ shall greatly rejoice when I sing to You" (Psalm 71:23)

13 "Let Your saints rejoice in _____" (2 Chronicles 6:41)

14 "The _____ shall rejoice and blossom as the rose" (Isaiah 35:1)

15 "I rejoice at Your _____ as one who finds great treasure" (Psalm 119:162)

16 "I will rejoice in Your _____" (Psalm 9:14)

17 "But let the righteous be glad; let them rejoice before God; yes, let them rejoice _____" (Psalm 68:3)

18 "In the shadow of Your _____ I will rejoice" (Psalm 63:7)

19 "The righteous shall rejoice when he sees the _____ [of the Lord]" (Psalm 58:10)

20 "Rejoice, O young man, in your _____" (Ecclesiastes 11:9)

21 "Let all those rejoice who put their _____ in You" (Psalm 5:11)

1 _ _ _ _ _

2 _ _ _ _ _

3

4 _ _ _ _

5 _ _ _ _ _ _

6 _ _ _ _

7

AGAIN | I | WILL SAY, REJOICE!

8 _ _ _ _

9 _ _ _ _

10 _ _ _ _ _ _ _

11 _ _ _ _

12 _ _ _ _

13 _ _ _ _ _ _

14 _ _ _ _ _ _

15 _ _ _ _ _

16 _ _ _ _

17 _ _ _ _ _ _

18 _ _ _ _

19 _ _ _ _ _ _

20 _ _ _ _ _

21 _ _ _ _ _ _

*T*he names of plants, birds, and animals in the Song of Solomon are the words you'll need to complete this crossword!

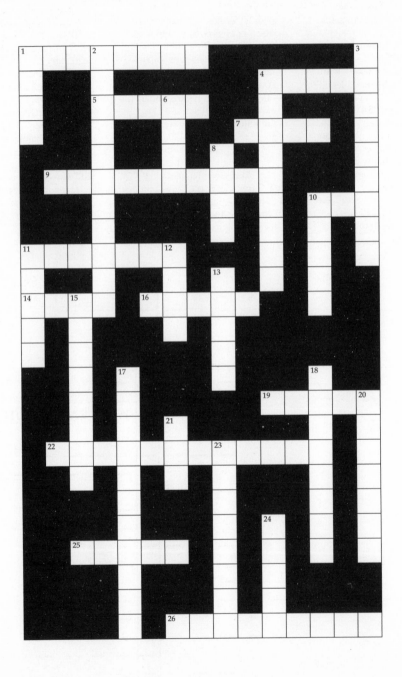

**Across**

1 Come with me from Lebanon . . .
rom the mountains of the _____
(4:8)

4 Your teeth are like a flock of shorn
_____ which have come up from
the washing (4:2)

5 A bundle of _____ is my beloved
to me (1:13)

7 Come with me from Lebanon . . .
from the _____s' dens (4:8)

9 The time of singing has come, and
the voice of the _____ is heard in
our land (2:12)

10 The beams of our houses are cedar,
and our rafters of _____ (1:17)

11 _____ and cinnamon (4:14)

14 My _____ , my perfect one (5:2)

16 His locks are wavy, and black as a
_____ (5:11)

19 Follow in the footsteps of the flock,
and feed your little _____ beside
the shepherds' tents (1:8)

22 With all the trees of _____ , myrrh
and aloes (4:14)

25 With all the trees of frankincense,
myrrh and _____ (4:14)

26 They made me the keeper of the
_____ , but my own . . . I have not
kept (1:6)

**Down**

1 Like a _____ among thorns, so is
my love among the daughters (2:2)

2 Your temples behind your veil are
like a piece of _____ (4:3)

3 Like an _____ among the trees of
the woods, so is my beloved among
the sons (2 words) (2:3)

4 _____ and saffron (4:14)

6 I am the _____ of Sharon (2:1)

8 I charge you, O daughters of
Jerusalem, by the gazelles or by the
_____ of the field (2:7)

10 Catch us the _____ . . . that spoil
the vines (2:15)

11 The beams of our houses are
_____ , and our rafters of fir (1:17)

12 My beloved is like a gazelle or a
young _____ (2:9)

13 His cheeks are like a bed of spices,
banks of scented _____ (5:13)

15 They made me the keeper of the
vineyards, but my own _____ I
have not kept (1:6)

17 My beloved is to me a cluster of
_____ _____ in the vineyards of
En Gedi (2 words) (1:14)

18 I charge you, O daughters of
Jerusalem, by the _____ or by the
does of the field, do not stir up nor
awaken love until it pleases (2:7)

20 Spikenard and _____ (4:14)

21 The _____ tree puts forth her green
figs (2:13)

23 Calamus and _____ (4:14)

24 I have compared you, my love, to
my _____ among Pharaoh's
chariots (1:9)

*I*n Job 38–39, the Lord spoke to Job out of a whirlwind and asked him a number of questions. Transfer the words that complete the questions below to the acrostic grid, and discover what was revealed to Job through these questions.

1 "Have you given the horse _____ ?" (39:19)

2 "Have you seen the treasury of _____ ?" (38:22)

3 "Who has divided a . . . path for the _____ ?" (38:25)

4 "Do you know the _____ when the wild mountain goats bear young?" (39:1)

5 "Where were you when I laid the _____ of the earth?" (38:4)

6 "Who laid its [the earth's] cornerstone, when . . . all the sons of God shouted for _____ ?" (38:6–7)

7 "Who shut in the _____ with doors …when I said, 'This far you may come, but no farther, and here your proud waves must stop!'" (38:8, 11)

8 "Who laid its [the earth's] cornerstone, when the _____ _____ sang together?" (2 words) (38:6–7)

9 "Have you seen the doors of the shadow of _____ ?" (38:17)

10 "And darkness, where is its place, that you may take it to its _____ ?" (38:19–20)

11 "Have you entered the treasury of _____ ?" (38:22)

12 "Who provides _____ for the raven?" (38:41)

13 "Who has divided a channel for the overflowing _____ ?" (38:25)

14 "Have you comprehended the _____ of the earth?" (38:18)

15 "From whose womb comes the _____ ?" (38:29)

16 "Have you . . . caused the _____ to know its place?" (38:12)

17 "Can you bind the cluster of the Pleiades, or _____ the belt of Orion?" (38:31)

18 "Who has put _____ in the mind?" (38:36)

19 "By what way is ... the east _____ scattered over the earth?" (38:24)

20 "By what way is _____ diffused?" (38:24)

21 "Can you send out _____ , that they may go, and say to you, 'Here we are!'?" (38:35)

22 "Who has given _____ to the heart?" (38:36)

23 "Where is the _____ to the dwelling or light?" (38:19)

24 "Have you entered the _____ of the sea?" (38:16)

25 "And the _____ of heaven, who gives it birth?" (38:29)

26 "Who has begotten the drops of _____ ?" (38:28)

1 _ _ _ _ _ _ _
2 _ _ _ _
3 _ _ _ _ _ _ _
4 _ _ _
5 _ _ _ _ _ _
6 _ _ _
7 _ _
8 _ _ _ _ _ _ _ _
9 _ _ _
10 _ _ _ _ _ _
11 _ _ _
12 _ _ _ _
13 _ _ _
14 _ _ _ _ _ _
15 _ _ _
16 _ _ _ _
17 _ _ _ _
18 _ _ _ _ _
19 _ _ _
20 _ _ _
21 _ _ _ _ _ _ _ _
22 _ _ _ _ _ _ _ _ _
23 _ _ _
24 _ _ _ _ _
25 _ _ _ _
26 _ _ _ _

# AN EXTRAVAGANT OFFERING

*A*fter encountering the Lord on Mount Sinai, Moses gathered all the children of Israel together and said, "These are the words which the LORD has commanded you to do" (Exodus 35:1). Moses went on to tell the people the Lord's plan for building a tabernacle, the ark of the covenant, and all the utensils and furnishings for the tabernacle.

The Scriptures tell us, "Then everyone came whose heart was stirred, and everyone whose spirit was willing, and they brought the LORD's offering for the work for the tabernacle of meeting, for all its service, and for the holy garments. They came, both men and women, as many as had a willing heart" (Exodus 35:21–22).

The people brought jewelry, yarn, fabrics, skins, and wood in such abundance that Moses eventually had to issue a proclamation, "Let neither man nor woman do any more work for the offering of the sanctuary" (Exodus 36:6–7). The people were restrained from bringing, for the material they had was sufficient for all the work to be done—indeed too much.

Start ↓

*O*h say, can you find the Bible *O* words to complete this crossword?

## Across

5 One of Naomi's daughters-in-law; she stayed behind when Naomi and Ruth returned to Judah (Ruth 1:4, 8–9, 14)

6 Caleb's nephew, he is described as a "deliverer for the children of Israel," raised up by the Lord (Judges 3:9–11)

9 "_____ and perfume delight the heart" (Proverbs 27:9)

11 Paul asked the Ephesians to pray "that I may _____ my mouth boldly to make known the mystery of the gospel" (Ephesians 6:19)

13 Either, _____

15 Ancient measurement, "one-tenth of an ephah" (Exodus 16:36)

16 The thirty-first book of the Bible

18 In John's Revelation, Jesus calls Himself the "Root and the _____ of David, the Bright and Morning Star" (Revelation 22:16)

19 Paul rejoiced to see the "good _____ and the steadfastness" of faith shown by the Colossians (Colossians 2:5)

20 The first believers are described as being "of _____ heart and _____ soul" (Acts 4:32)

22 The king of Bashan defeated by the children of Israel; he was a giant with an iron bed nine cubits long (Deuteronomy 3:11)

23 Elder, opposite of younger; Joseph was Benjamin's _____ brother (Genesis 35:24)

24 A gift to God; a lamb or kid was used as a "sin _____" by the children of Israel (Leviticus 5:5–6)

26 After the Last Supper, Matthew says the disciples sang a hymn and went to the Mount of _____ (Matthew 26:30)

27 "_____ , that the salvation of Israel would come out of Zion" (Psalm 14:7)

28 One of Judah's sons who died in the land of Canaan (Genesis 46:12)

29 Jesus was displeased to find moneychangers selling "_____ and sheep and doves" in the temple (John 2:14–15)

31 The Lord saw that the thoughts of men's hearts—except for Noah's—were "_____ evil continually" (Genesis 6:5, 8)

32 Evil king of Israel, he bought the hill of Shemer and built a city called Samaria; Ahab was his son (1 Kings 16:16–28)

33 "The wings of the _____ wave proudly, but . . . God deprived her of wisdom" (Job 39:13, 17)

34 Opposite of off; also the name of one of Reuben's grandsons (Numbers 16:1)

35 As they walked in the wilderness, the children of Israel craved "the cucumbers, the melons, the leeks, the _____ , and the garlic" of Egypt (Numbers 11:5)

37 Paul called the Gentiles "a wild _____ tree" grafted in among the Jews (Romans 11:17)

39 Paul wrote that Titus's "affections are greater for you as he remembers the _____ of you all" (2 Corinthians 7:15)

42 The Lord promised to heal the wounds of His people "because they called you an _____" (Jeremiah 30:17)

44 Jeremiah commanded the people not to "_____ the stranger, the fatherless, and the widow" (Jeremiah 7:6)

45 "God created man in His _____ image" (Genesis 1:27)

46 The Lord said to the church of Ephesus, "To him who _____ I will give to eat from the tree of life" (Revelation 2:7)

**Down**

1 A region known for its gold (Job 22:24)

2 Philemon's runaway servant (Philemon 10–11)

3 The psalmist said, "I have been young, and now am _____ ; yet I have not seen the righteous forsaken" (Psalm 37:25)

4 Jesus told His disciples to make disciples of all nations, "teaching them to _____ all things that I have commanded you" (Matthew 28:20)

6 The centurion believed the "_____ of the ship" more than Paul, and the ship sank as Paul had prophesied (Acts 27:9–44)

7 Fragrance, aroma from sacrifices

8 Alpha and _____ , the Beginning and the End (Revelation 22:13)

10 "All who handle the _____ , the mariners . . . will make their voice heard because of you" (Ezekiel 27:29–30)

12 A town of the tribe of Benjamin (Nehemiah 11:31–35)

13 The psalmist said, "You shall make them [enemies] as a fiery _____ in the time of Your anger" (Psalm 21:9)

14 A prophet of the Lord who cried out against the people of Judah's being taken captive (2 Chronicles 28:9–11)

17 Opposite of on

19 Jesus said it would be better for a person to have a millstone hung around his neck and be thrown into the sea than to "_____ one of these little ones" (Luke 17:2)

20 "Fatherless" children; "We have become _____ and waifs, our mothers are like widows" (Lamentations 5:3)

21 Type of stones engraved with the names of the twelve tribes of Israel and placed on the shoulders of the priest's holy garment (Exodus 39:6–7)

22 The prophet Samuel "took a flask of _____ " and poured it over Saul's head to anoint him (1 Samuel 10:1)

23 Son of Naomi and Boaz, he was King David's grandfather (Ruth 4:13, 17)

25 Samuel said, "To _____ is better than sacrifice, and to heed than the fat of rams" (1 Samuel 15:22)

26 Paul said this man often refreshed him and was not ashamed of his prisoner's chains (2 Timothy 1:16)

29 The Lord "made the Pleiades and _____ " according to the prophet Amos (Amos 5:8)

30 Ahithophel's evil advice to Absalom was regarded "as if one had inquired at the _____ of God"—but he hadn't! (2 Samuel 16:23)

32 All powerful; nature of God

35 Elijah asked the people, "How long will you falter between two _____ ?" (1 Kings 18:21)

36 "I made myself gardens and _____ , and I planted all kinds of fruit trees in them" said the preacher in Ecclesiastes 2:5

38 "For men indeed swear by the greater, and an _____ for confirmation is for them an end of all dispute" (Hebrews 6:16)

40 The craftsman "takes the cypress and the _____ ; he secures it for himself among the trees of the forest" (Isaiah 44:14)

41 Place of refreshment and water in a desert

43 Sixth son of Jesse (1 Chronicles 2:15)

# VISIT TO ELIZABETH

*W*hen the angel Gabriel came to Mary and announced to her, "You will conceive in your womb and bring forth a Son, and shall call His name Jesus," the angel also told Mary, "Elizabeth your relative has also conceived a son in her old age; and this is now the sixth month for her who was called barren. For with God nothing will be impossible" (Luke 1:31, 36–37).

After the angel departed, Mary went immediately to the hill country of Judah to the home of Zacharias and Elizabeth. When Elizabeth heard the greeting of Mary, the babe in her womb leaped and Elizabeth was filled with the Holy Spirit. She cried out to Mary, "Blessed are you among women, and blessed is the fruit of your womb! But why is this granted to me, that the mother of my Lord should come to me?" (Luke 1:42–43)

Both women received confirmation from the other about the miracle babies they were carrying.

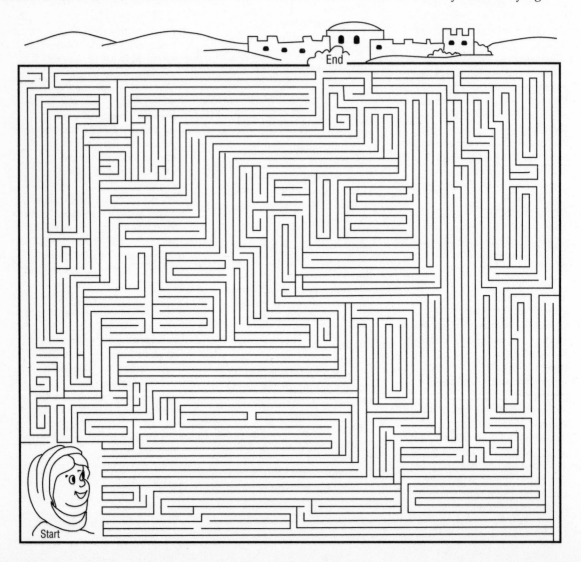

*J*esus is associated with various "numbers" of things, people, days, years, and "times" in His ministry. Complete the equation below to get to a major truth stated by the Lord. (Work down the first column; then continue to the second.)

The number of people Jesus fed with five loaves and two fishes (Luke 9:13–16)   =  ____

Minus . . .
Number of people Jesus fed from seven loaves (Mark 8:1–9)   −  ____

Divided by . . .
Number of virgins who were "wise" in parable (Matthew 25:2)   ÷  ____

Multiplied by . . .
Number of times Jesus said Peter would deny Him (Matthew 26:75)   ×  ____

Minus . . .
Number of times Jesus said we are to forgive (Matthew 18:22)
(____ × ____ =)   −  ____

Minus . . .
Number of appointed ones sent out by Jesus to Judean cities; they returned saying "even the demons are subject to us in Your name" (Luke 10:17)   −  ____

Multiplied by . . .
Number of apostles still alive at the time of Jesus' resurrection (Mark 16:14)   ×  ____

Minus . . .
Number of days Jesus fasted in the wilderness (Matthew 4:2)   −  ____

Divided by . . .
Number of sheep the shepherd had before losing one (in parable) (Luke 15:4)   ÷  ____

Multiplied by . . .
Number of lepers healed by Jesus (Luke 17:12)   ×  ____

Minus . . .
Number of healed lepers who returned to give thanks (Luke 17:15)   −  ____

Plus . . .
Number of years the man at the Pool of Bethesda had been ill when Jesus healed him (John 5:5)   +  ____

Plus . . .
Number of disciples Jesus took with Him to raise the daughter of Jairus (Luke 8:51)   +  ____

Minus . . .
Number of years a woman had a flow of blood before being healed by Jesus (Luke 8:43)   −  ____

Minus . . .
Minimum return of good seed planted in good soil: ____ fold (Matthew 13:23)   −  ____

Minus . . .
Number of years woman had been bent over with an infirmity before being healed by Jesus (Luke 13:11)   −  ____

Minus . . .
Day of circumcision of newborn son after birth (Luke 2:21)   −  ____

Divided by . . .
Age of Jesus at the time He stayed behind in Jerusalem to be about His Father's business (Luke 2:42–49)   ÷  ____

Equals . . .
The nature of Jesus and His Father (John 10:30)   =  ____

*F*ill in the blanks of Psalm 98 to complete this crossword!

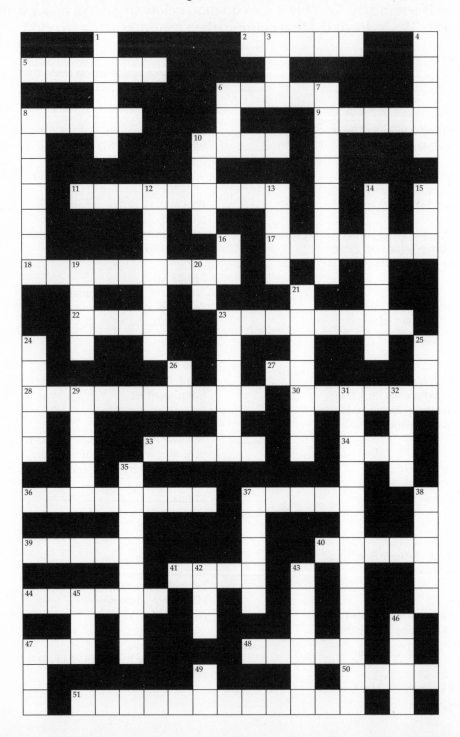

_____ , _____ _____ the LORD a
20 Down    50 Across   27 Across

new _____ ! For He has done _____
13 Down                11 Across

things; His _____ hand and _____
9 Across         15 Down

_____ arm have _____ _____
10 Down         44 Across   47 Down

the _____ . The _____ _____
12 Down     19 Down   47 Across

made known His _____ ; His
18 Across

_____ He has _____ in the _____
31 Down        23 Across       37 Across

of the _____ . He has _____ His
17 Across        28 Across

_____ and His _____ to the
29 Down         51 Across

_____ of _____ ; all the _____ of
33 Across   30 Across         32 Down

the _____ have seen the salvation of
4 Down

_____ _____ . _____ _____ to
42 Down   34 Across   6 Across   36 Across

the LORD, _____ the earth; break
25 Down

_____ in song, _____ , and sing
24 Down        21 Down

_____ . Sing to the LORD with the
8 Down

_____ , with the harp and the _____
10 Across                 37 Down

of a _____ , with _____ and the
8 Across         7 Down

sound _____ a _____ ; shout
49 Down     41 Across

joyfully before the LORD, the _____ .
46 Down

Let the _____ _____ , and all
6 Down    22 Across

_____ _____ , the world and
45 Down    35 Down

_____ _____ _____ _____ it;
48 Across   3 Down   2 Across   16 Down

let the _____ clap their hands; let the
23 Down

_____ _____ joyful together
1 Down    26 Down

_____ the LORD, for He is coming to
43 Down

_____ the earth. With righteousness
38 Down

He _____ judge the _____ , and the
39 Across         40 Across

_____ with _____ .
14 Down     5 Across

## Word Pool

ALL BE BEFORE DWELL EARTH ENDS EQUITY FAITHFULNESS FORTH FULLNESS
GAINED GOD HARP HAS HILLS HIM HIS HOLY HORN HOUSE IN ISRAEL
ITS JOYFULLY JUDGE KING LORD MARVELOUS MERCY NATIONS OF OH OUR
PEOPLES PRAISES PSALM REJOICE REMEMBERED REVEALED RIGHT
RIGHTEOUSNESS RIVERS ROAR SALVATION SEA SHALL SHOUT SIGHT SING SONG
SOUND THOSE TO TRUMPETS VICTORY WHO WORLD

*A*ccording to early church history, believers in Rome during the first century often met in the City's catacombs—a series of underground burial chambers and sarcophagi. How long will it take you to find your way to the meeting of Christians through this catacomb maze?

**Start**

*S*ee if you can work out these words of Jesus before it's time to eat.

*Clue:* MESSIAH *is* PSHHQDN

P Z    C B B T    Q H    L B

T B    L N S    G Q E E    B C

N Q P    G N B    H S J L    P S '

D J T    L B    C Q J Q H N

N Q H    G B K I .

21

*I*n the final days before His death and resurrection, Jesus instituted the Lord's Supper as a sign of the new covenant. Fill in the blanks below and the circled letters will tell you how we are to take the Lord's Supper.

1 "This is My _____ which is broken for you" (1 Corinthians 11:24)

2 This bread symbolized the continual presence of God (Exodus 25:30)

3 "Take, _____ "(Matthew 26:26)

4 The One who gives the true bread (John 6:32)

5 "He who eats My flesh and drinks My blood _____ in Me, and I in him" (John 6:56)

6 "My _____ is food indeed" (John 6:55)

7 "He took the cup . . . saying, '_____ from it'" (Matthew 26:27)

8 "I am the _____ bread" (John 6:51)

9 "Whoever eats My flesh and drinks My blood has _____ _____ " (2 words) (John 6:54)

10 Where the disciples ate the Last Supper (2 words) (Luke 22:12)

11 "Let a man _____ himself, and so let him eat of the bread and drink of the cup" (1 Corinthians 11:28)

12 "This is My blood of the _____ _____ " (2 words) (Matthew 26:28)

13 The bread we break is the _____ of the body of Christ (1 Corinthians 10:16)

14 "My _____ is drink indeed" (John 6:55)

15 "He who eats this bread will live _____ " (John 6:58)

16 This bread is eaten at Passover (Exodus 12:8)

17 "He who comes to Me shall never _____ " (John 6:35)

18 "For as often as you eat this bread and drink this cup, you _____ the Lord's death till He comes" (1 Corinthians 11:26)

19 "He took bread, _____ _____ and broke it"(2 words) (Luke 22:19)

20 The Last Supper was during the time of the _____ (Luke 22:1, 11)

21 "Unless you eat the flesh of the Son of Man and drink His blood, you have no _____ in you" (John 6:53)

22 "My blood . . . for the _____ of sins" (Matthew 26:28)

23 "Jesus took _____ , blessed and broke it, and gave it to the disciples" (Matthew 26:26)

1
2
3
4
5
6
7
8
9
10
11
12
13
14
15
16
17
18
19
20
21
22
23

*T*he answers to this puzzle will "ring true". . . when you get them correct.

## Across

1 Fact
6 The good news
11 Echo
13 Hawaiian feast
14 Sentinel
15 "And you shall know the truth, and the truth shall make you _____ " (John 8:32)
17 Arachnid
19 Velocity
21 Maple syrup state (abbr.)
22 Balance beam specialist
23 "_____ into all the world" (Mark 16:15)
25 Half of IV
26 Unlock
28 Respite
31 Russian ruler
33 "Just _____ I Am"
34 Behave
35 Place to find a needle?
38 Tribunal
41 Capital of Norway
42 Attention
45 Crowd
47 Pedro's aunt
48 Buckeye state
50 Winter sport
51 "The truth of the LORD _____ forever" (Psalm 117:2)
53 GB's presidential predecessor (initials)
54 Flush
55 "Rightly dividing the _____ of truth" (2 Timothy 2:15)

## Down

1 Faith
2 _____ what you sow
3 Honorable
4 Nickname for a president or a bear
5 Half a laugh
6 Word listing
7 School in Norman, Oklahoma (initials)
8 Secure
9 Unsullied
10 Confederate leader, Robert E. _____
12 Oxidize
16 Brink
18 Give off
20 Kennedy book, _____ 109

21 Accuracy
24 Off's opposite
26 Dinner for a horse
27 A Bible book that includes many prayers
29 Short for finance course
30 Stammer
32 Large U.S. airline (initials)
36 One voice
37 Stew or bake
39 Horse restraint
40 Exchange
43 Wound
44 That was _____ ; this is now
46 Sparrow
49 Verb of being
52 Between T and W

*J*esus gave an important message about time to His disciples as they awaited the Day of the Lord.

### *Clue:* MESSIAH *is* ZRFFVNU

U R N I R A     N A Q     R N E G U

J V Y Y     C N F F     N J N L'     O H G     Z L

J B E Q F     J V Y Y     O L     A B     Z R N A F

C N F F     N J N L.     O H G     B S     G U N G

Q N L     N A Q     U B H E     A B     B A R

X A B J F'     A B G     R I R A     G U R

N A T R Y F     V A     U R N I R A'

A B E     G U R     F B A'     O H G

B A Y L     G U R     S N G U R E.

# CRUX ANSATA

*T*he Crux Ansata is of early Egyptian origin. It combines the Greek letter *tau* (which looks like a *T*) with a loop above it that symbolizes completeness or wholeness.

Can you tell what time of day is being described from these clues? Do you know what is reported as happening in the Scriptures during that time period? (Remember that while the Jewish day began at dusk, the "first hour" in telling time at dawn was about 6 A.M.)

## Clues

It was about opposite the time of day when Jesus walked on the water (Matthew 14:25).

Well before the time when Nicodemus came to see Jesus (John 3:2).

And even before Jesus went by Himself to pray after feeding the five thousand (Matthew 14:23).

It was well after, however, the time when the women came to the tomb after Jesus' crucifixion (Matthew 28:1).

And after the time when Jesus arrived in the temple to teach (John 8:2).

It was before the hour when Jesus was asked, "Where are You staying?" and the disciples remained with Him when He offered, "Come and see" (John 1:36–39).

But after the hour of His crucifixion (Mark 15:25).

In fact, it ended at the same hour when Jesus cried out from the cross, "My God, My God, why have You forsaken Me?" (Mark 15:34).

And began at the same hour when Jesus sat by the well at Sychar (John 4:6).

## Answer

The time period is _____

The event that happened during this time period was

_____

# EASTER LILIES

The word *lily* in the Scriptures may refer to a number of different flowers, from Madonna lilies to hyacinths. It may be a generic term for describing any brightly colored flower.

The lilies that decorated Solomon's temple were probably modeled after the water lily, or lotus. This was a common architectural motif in Egypt, Persia, and Assyria. (See 1 Kings 7:19–26.)

Jesus said, "Consider the lilies, how they grow: they neither toil nor spin; and yet I say to you, even Solomon in all his glory was not arrayed like one of these. If then God so clothes the grass, which today is in the field and tomorrow is thrown into the oven, how much more will He clothe you, O you of little faith?" (Luke 12:27–28). The lilies to which Jesus was referring were probably wild *Anemone coronaria*, a bright purple flower that still grows freely on the hillsides around the Sea of Galilee.

Lilies have become a common Easter symbol primarily because they are nearly always in bloom at Easter.

*I*n the words of the Fanny Crosby hymn, "Redeemed and so happy in Jesus, no language my rapture can tell." Redeemed! Redeemed!

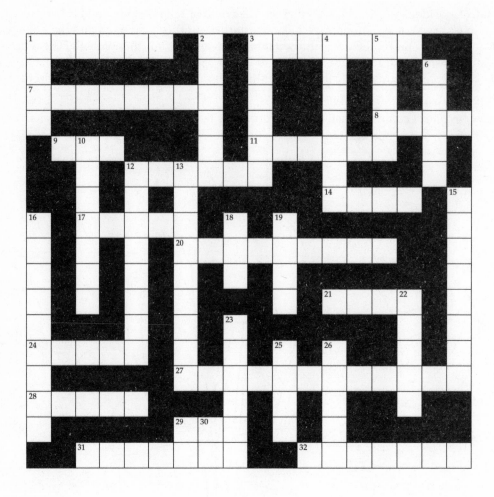

**Across**

1 In His mercy, God led forth the "populace" He redeemed from Pharaoh (Exodus 15:13)

3 His blood redeemed us and made us kings and _____ to our God (Revelation 5:9–10)

7 "Redeem Israel, O God, out of all their 'difficulties'" (Psalm 25:22)

8 He redeemed Naomi's land (Ruth 4:8–10)

9 God redeemed Israel with an outstretched _____ (Exodus 6:6)

11 In a period of "no food," He redeems us from death (Job 5:20)

12 The Lord brought the Israelites out with a "powerful" hand (Deuteronomy 7:8)

14 My _____ , which God has redeemed, will rejoice, said the psalmist (Psalm 71:23)

17 Christ redeemed us from the "plague" of the law (Galatians 3:13)

20 The Lord redeemed David's life from "affliction" (2 Samuel 4:9)

21 Every firstborn of a donkey was redeemed with a _____ (Exodus 13:13)

24 The "Heavenly Being" redeemed Israel from all evil (Genesis 48:16)

27 We weren't redeemed with "corruptible things, like _____ _____ _____ " (3 words) (1 Peter 1:18)

28 God redeemed the Israelites from slavery in this land (Deuteronomy 15:15)

29 Ephraim and Samaria, though redeemed, spoke "falsehoods" (sing.) against God (Hosea 7:13)

31 Zacharias said God had "called on" and redeemed His people (Luke 1:68)

32 The rich can't redeem this sibling (Psalm 49:6–7)

**Down**

1 He redeemed His children in His love and "compassion" (Isaiah 63:9)

2 He redeemed His people, the sons of Jacob and _____ (Psalm 77:15)

3 He redeemed us from lawless deeds and "refines" (sing.) for Himself His own special people (Titus 2:14)

4 Redeem my soul and deliver me because of my "foes," said David (Psalm 69:18)

5 Asaph urged God to remember the "clan" of His inheritance, which He had redeemed (Psalm 74:2)

6 The sons of Korah were redeemed from the power of the "burial plot" (Psalm 49:15)

10 Another word for redeemed (Psalm 136:24)

12 "Redeem me and be 'compassionate' to me," was David's plea (Psalm 26:11)

13 Moses pleaded, "Don't destroy those You redeemed through Your 'eminence'" (Deuteronomy 9:26)

15 The "bought back" of the Lord shall return and come to Zion, singing (Isaiah 51:11)

16 The Lord has redeemed this city of righteousness, Isaiah said (Isaiah 52:9)

18 _____ *Maria*

19 I'll redeem you from the "clutch" of the terrible, God told Jeremiah (Jeremiah 15:21)

22 "In Him we have redemption through His _____ " (Ephesians 1:7)

23 A man had a year to redeem a house he sold in this type of city (Leviticus 25:29)

25 "And the 'twelve months' of My redeemed has come" (Isaiah 63:4)

26 God redeemed His people by His great "strength" (Nehemiah 1:10)

29 Lieutenant (abbr.)

30 That is (abbr.)

# THE RUSSIAN CROSS

*T*he Russian Cross, also called the Eastern Cross or the Slavic Cross, appears on the tombs of the early czars and it also is seen frequently on the spire or dome of the Eastern Orthodox Church.

The upper bar indicates the inscription that Pilate wrote about Jesus, "JESUS OF NAZARETH, THE KING OF THE JEWS" (John 19:19). The lower slanted bar is said to have been the footrest of the cross. The Eastern Church believed that Jesus was crucified with His feet side by side, rather than one over the other, as seen in early paintings of the Western Church.

The reason for the slant of the lower bar is a mystery. One tradition says that the earthquake at the time of the crucifixion caused the bar to slant. A more probable theory is that the lower bar forms the shape of the Cross Saltire or St. Andrew's Cross (see *St. Andrew's Cross* maze). Andrew is the apostle who is believed to have introduced Christianity into Russia.

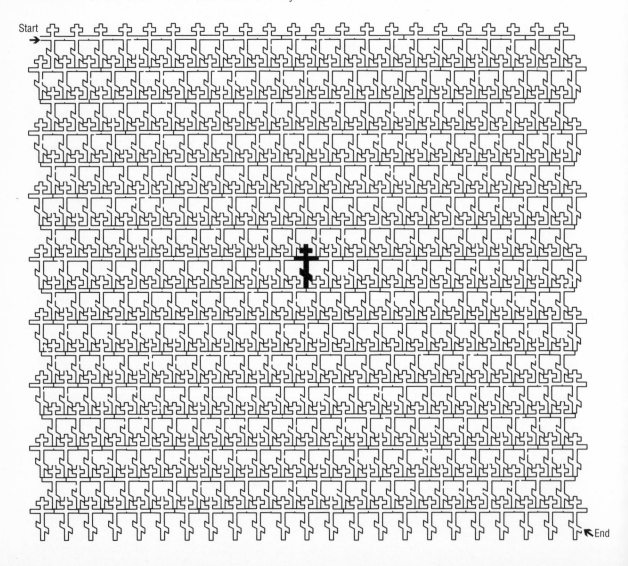

Start →

End

*I*n the letter box below, find the "companion" word in these common groupings of words from the Bible.

Trust and _____
Adam and _____
Peter, James, and _____
The Law and the _____
The Way, the Truth, and the _____
Abraham and _____
Cain and _____
Jonathan and _____
Faith, Hope, and _____
Father, Son, and _____ _____ (2 words)

Kingdom, Power, and _____
Shadrach, Meshach, and _____
Samson and _____
Abraham, Isaac, and _____
Heaven and _____
Life and _____
Grace and _____
Now and _____
Body and _____
Good and _____

| | | | | | | | | | | | | | | |
|---|---|---|---|---|---|---|---|---|---|---|---|---|---|---|
| G | D | L | P | E | A | F | O | R | B | L | O | A | B | E | D | E |
| A | B | E | V | D | E | L | C | A | J | B | S | A | R | S | V | N |
| D | A | V | E | I | D | E | A | T | B | L | E | B | A | I | G | O |
| B | E | D | A | V | E | G | O | G | H | O | P | F | L | P | R | O |
| P | H | V | E | A | T | S | B | L | O | E | H | V | I | O | F | L |
| S | A | B | E | D | N | E | G | O | S | O | P | R | A | H | O | I |
| D | E | L | I | A | H | J | A | R | L | O | V | E | V | I | R | D |
| P | R | O | P | H | O | E | H | Y | T | S | F | J | A | P | E | C |
| E | B | O | C | A | J | A | S | A | C | I | J | O | H | C | V | H |
| E | H | V | E | O | B | P | E | Y | L | A | B | E | H | D | E | N |
| G | A | L | O | R | I | Y | H | O | L | E | S | E | T | P | R | I |
| I | R | I | T | R | S | L | O | V | Y | P | L | V | A | C | E | F |
| H | A | L | I | L | E | D | R | E | V | L | R | E | E | L | L | H |
| A | S | T | E | H | P | O | R | P | J | A | C | A | D | E | G | O |
| B | E | D | N | E | L | A | H | E | L | D | E | A | T | V | I | L |
| E | V | H | N | S | E | R | A | H | E | L | B | D | A | L | L | G |

*O*n especially stressful days, it's important to remember what the Bible says about "rest"—a scriptural concept that means not only relaxation but peace of spirit and freedom from oppression.

Complete the verses below—which reveal vital, stress-free benefits—and use the missing words to fill in the acrostic grid. You'll discover an important command of God worth remembering!

1 "My Presence will go with you, and I will give you _____" (Exodus 33:14)

2 "Then the churches throughout all Judea, Galilee, and Samaria had peace and were _____" (Acts 9:31)

3 "Go, return each to her _____ house . . . The LORD grant that you may find rest" (Ruth 1:8–9)

4 "When the LORD your God has given you rest from your _____ all around, . . . you will blot out the remembrance of Amalek" (Deuteronomy 25:19)

5 "Sit still, my daughter, until you know how the _____ will turn out" (Ruth 3:18)

6 "You shall pass before your _____ armed, all your mighty men of valor, and help them, until the LORD has given your _____ rest, as He gave you" (Joshua 1:14–15)

7 "And to whom did He swear that they would not enter His rest, but to those who did not obey? So we see that they could not _____ in because of unbelief" (Hebrews 3:18–19)

8 "In that day there shall be a Root of Jesse, . . . and His _____ place shall be glorious" (Isaiah 11:10)

9 "It is a righteous thing with God to repay with _____ those who trouble you, and to give you who are troubled rest" (2 Thessalonians 1:6–7)

10 "Tomorrow is a Sabbath rest, a _____ Sabbath to the LORD" (Exodus 16:23)

11 "Then the land shall rest and _____ its sabbaths" (Leviticus 26:34)

12 "Work shall be done for six days, but the _____ is the Sabbath of rest" (Exodus 31:15)

13 "I would have been _____ ; then I would have been at rest" (Job 3:13)

14 "If you would prepare your heart, and stretch out your hands toward Him; . . . you would be secure, _____ there is hope" (Job 11:13, 18)

15 "Return to your rest, O my soul, for the LORD has dealt _____ with you" (Psalm 116:7)

16 "Blessed is the man whom You instruct, O LORD . . . that You may give him rest from the days of _____ " (Psalm 94:12–13)

17 "I am not at ease, nor am I quiet; I have no rest, for _____ comes" (Job 3:26)

18 "The LORD blessed the Sabbath day and _____ it" (Exodus 20:11)

19 "Oh, that I had wings like a _____ ! I would fly away and be at rest" (Psalm 55:6)

20 "Arise, O LORD, to Your resting place, You and the _____ of Your strength" (Psalm 132:8)

21 "Take My _____ upon you and learn from Me, for I am gentle and lowly in heart, and you will find rest for your souls" (Matthew 11:29)

```
 1  __  __  __  __
 2  __  __  __  __  __  __  __
 3  __  __  __  __  __  __
 4  __  __  __  __  __
 5  __  __  __  __
 6  __  __  __  __  __                __
 7  __  __  __  __  __
 8  __  __  __  __  __
 9  __  __  __  __  __  __        __  __  __  __
10  __  __  __  __
11  __  __  __  __  __
12  __  __  __  __  __  __
13  __  __  __  __  __
14  __  __  __  __  __  __
15  __  __  __  __  __            __  __  __
16  __  __  __  __          __  __
17  __  __  __
18  __  __  __  __  __        __
19  __  __  __
20  __  __  __
21  __  __  __
```

*In* each father-son pair below, the name of either the son or the father has been scrambled. Unscramble these names and then unscramble the circled letters to reveal an important scriptural bond in a father-son relationship.

| FATHER | SON | |
|---|---|---|
| ABRAHAM | CSAIA | Ⓞ _ _ _ _ |
| HEUJ | JEHOAHAZ | _ Ⓞ _ _ |
| ONHA | SHEM | Ⓞ _ _ _ |
| DAVID | LOOMSNO | _ _ _ _ _ _ Ⓞ |
| ASA | SOEJHAHTAHP | _ _ _ _ _ _ _ Ⓞ _ _ |
| MARAM | MOSES | _ _ Ⓞ _ _ |
| AMAZIAH | AZIHARA | _ _ _ _ Ⓞ _ _ |
| EHPETUL | JOEL | _ _ Ⓞ _ _ _ |
| AARON | LEERAAZ | _ _ _ Ⓞ _ _ |
| ISAAC | BAJCO | _ _ Ⓞ _ _ |
| SEEJS | DAVID | _ Ⓞ _ _ _ |

Unscrambled the circled letters here:

_ _ _ _ _ _ _ _ _ _ _

*T*his crossword is about one of the most valued entities in the Bible—both literally and spiritually—LIGHT!

## Across

2 Second Samuel 23:4 says that the Messiah "shall be like the light of the morning when the _____ rises"

3 "They _____ in the dark without light, and He makes them stagger like a drunken man," says Job 12:25

5 "Light is _____ for the righteous, and gladness for the upright in heart," says Psalm 97:11

7 Isaiah said of the Messiah, "The people who _____ in darkness have seen a great light" (Isaiah 9:2)

8 "The light of the _____ indeed goes out," says Job 18:5

12 God said, "Let there be lights in the _____ of the heavens to divide the day from the night" (Genesis 1:14)

13 The "lesser light" (Genesis 1:16)

14 "Truly the light is _____ , and it is pleasant for the eyes to behold the sun" (Ecclesiastes 11:7)

15 The arrival of day

19 After Mordecai's victory over Haman, Esther's people experienced "light and _____ , joy and honor" (Esther 8:16)

21 As Paul traveled to Damascus "at about _____ , suddenly a great light from heaven shone around" him (Acts 22:6)

23 Intermittent bursting of light

24 The best place for Light to shine

25 Shining heat

26 Jesus said true believers do not "light a _____ and put it under a basket" (Matthew 5:15)

27 Jesus taught, "The lamp of the body is the _____ " (Matthew 6:22)

29 Jesus said, "While you have the light, _____ in the light, that you may become sons of light" (John 12:36)

30 The flame of the wicked "does not _____ " (Job 18:5)

31 "God made _____ great lights; the greater light to rule the day, and the lesser light to rule the night" (Genesis 1:16)

34 A faint or brief glow of light (especially in the eyes)

35 Offering to be given for light in the tabernacle (Exodus 35:28)

36 Habakkuk said, "The sun and moon stood still in their habitation; at the light of Your _____ " (Habakkuk 3:11)

37 Opposite of night

## Down

1 To fill or flood with light

2 "The light of the sun will be _____ , as the light of seven days," says Isaiah 30:26

4 The Lord led His people with a _____ of cloud by day and a _____ of fire by night (Exodus 13:21)

6 The Lord "knows what is in the _____ , and light dwells with Him" (Daniel 2:22)

9 During the plague of darkness, the Israelites in Egypt still had light in their _____ (Exodus 10:23)

10 Beam of light

11 During the Transfiguration, Jesus' clothes "became shining, exceedingly white, like _____ " (Mark 9:3)

12 God told Moses to take his sandals off his _____ in the presence of a bush that was burning but was not consumed (Exodus 3:1–5)

16 In the face of a night far spent, Paul encouraged the Romans to cast off the works of darkness, and "put on the _____ of light" (Romans 13:12)

17 The Lord asked Job where he was "when the morning stars _____ together" (Job 38:7)

18 In Isaiah's prophecy about the Messiah, he said that a light has shined on "those who dwelt in the land of the _____ of death" (Isaiah 9:2)

19 Habakkuk speaks of the sun and moon's standing still "at the shining of Your _____ spear" (Habakkuk 3:11)

20 The psalmist declared, "The LORD is my light and my _____ " (Psalm 27:1)

22 Opposite of day

25 A flicker of light

28 God began His creation by saying, " _____ there be light" (Genesis 1:3)

29 Shaft of sunlight or moonlight

32 Jesus said, " _____ while you have the light, lest darkness overtake you" (John 12:35)

33 After the defeat of Haman, the Jews had "light and gladness, _____ and honor" (Esther 8:16)

Find ten items in the box of letters below that were carried in baskets in the Bible.

```
B  G  O  O  S  K  A  B  N  E  V  A  E  L  N  U  E
A  D  T  V  A  E  U  L  T  M  M  U  S  H  D  B  D
K  E  N  E  S  A  L  E  A  I  E  F  H  E  A  R  E
M  O  O  D  E  T  M  S  G  R  U  R  F  A  E  S  A
E  T  G  D  B  N  F  R  T  T  F  G  I  F  R  I  F
A  D  S  O  A  E  G  A  I  S  U  M  S  M  B  E  R
P  O  O  U  K  M  S  A  U  L  B  R  H  F  D  U  H
R  G  T  A  E  M  A  B  R  M  H  E  A  I  E  N  E
O  D  M  M  D  E  K  S  F  I  S  U  S  D  N  L  A
D  E  P  E  G  D  D  I  R  R  I  S  G  A  E  E  F
U  R  M  R  O  A  G  R  E  E  A  M  M  R  V  A  R
C  E  U  F  O  S  F  R  M  C  T  G  E  B  A  V  A
F  M  S  R  D  D  H  U  M  L  I  U  M  D  E  N  G
I  G  U  A  S  F  U  E  U  A  W  R  F  E  L  U  M
T  I  E  H  I  D  E  C  S  X  T  F  E  C  N  S  B
F  H  A  S  S  A  D  D  E  R  U  E  D  U  U  T  A
I  U  P  R  E  R  B  O  C  E  I  P  O  R  P  D  S
S  U  N  L  E  A  V  U  R  U  T  I  U  R  S  E  K
```

**Scripture Pool**
GENESIS 40:17   LEVITICUS 8:2   DEUTERONOMY 26:2   JUDGES 6:19
2 KINGS 10:7   JEREMIAH 24:1   AMOS 8:2   MARK 6:43; 8:19   ACTS 9:24–25

# CROWN OF THORNS

*T*he crown of thorns is indicative of both the pain and the mockery associated with the crucifixion of Jesus.

The Scriptures tell us that Pilate's soldiers "took Jesus into the Praetorium and gathered the whole garrison around Him. And they stripped Him and put a scarlet robe on Him. When they had twisted a crown of thorns, they put it on His head, and a reed in His right hand. And they bowed the knee before Him and mocked Him, saying, 'Hail, King of the Jews!' Then they spat on Him, and took the reed and struck Him on the head. And when they had mocked Him, they took the robe off Him, put His own clothes on Him, and led Him away to be crucified" (Matthew 27:27–31).

Pilate commanded an inscription for the cross, "JESUS OF NAZARETH, THE KING OF THE JEWS," and had it written in Hebrew, Greek, and Latin (John 19:19). "Therefore the chief priests of the Jews said to Pilate, 'Do not write, "The King of the Jews," but, "He said, 'I am the King of the Jews.'"' Pilate answered, 'What I have written, I have written'" (v. 21–22).

Never was a crown more royal.

*It*'s hard to forgive someone who has hurt us. But forgiveness from God makes us realize its importance.

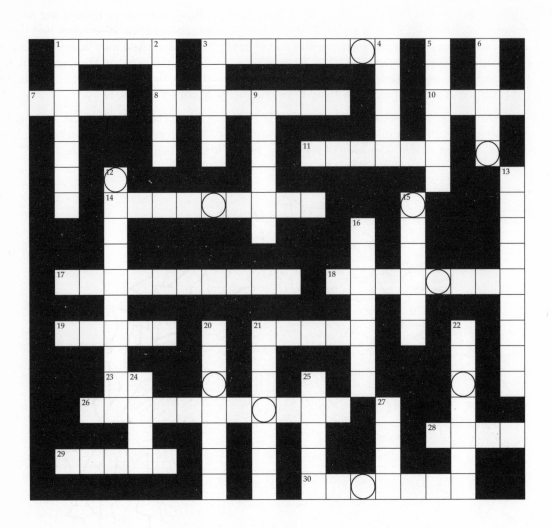

Bonus:

Unscramble the circled letters
to reveal what puts us into a position
to receive God's forgiveness.

— — — — — — — — —

## Across

1 Forgive seventy times _____ (Matthew 18:21–22)

3 Joseph forgave them (Genesis 45:3–5)

7 God would "mend" Israel's backsliding (Hosea 14:4)

8 God "erases" our transgressions (2 words) (Isaiah 43:25)

10 "Look on . . . my 'discomfort,' and forgive all my sins," said David (Psalm 25:18)

11 God will abundantly "excuse" (Isaiah 55:7)

14 Hezekiah requested "redemption" for the people (2 Chronicles 30:18)

17 "Forgive men their _____" (Matthew 6:14)

18 Whoever "trusts" in Him receives forgiveness (Acts 10:43)

19 The people worship "images"; don't forgive them, said Isaiah (Isaiah 2:8–9)

21 Those whose lawless "acts" are forgiven are fortunate (Romans 4:7)

23 _____ Shaddai

26 The sins of the woman who poured this on Jesus were forgiven (2 words) (Luke 7:46–47)

28 Once forgiven, the paralytic did this (Luke 5:23–25)

29 God is "prepared" to forgive (Psalm 86:5)

30 This great city sought forgiveness just in time (Jonah 3:5–10)

## Down

1 A martyr who forgave his killers (Acts 7:59–60)

2 Abigail, wife of _____ , begged David's forgiveness (1 Samuel 25:23–28)

3 Without shedding of this, there's no forgiveness (Hebrews 9:22)

4 If God marks iniquities, who can "remain upright"? (Psalm 130:3)

5 Ask for forgiveness (Acts 2:38)

6 We were dead in trespasses; now forgiven, we're _____ (Colossians 2:13)

9 This son of Gera confessed his sin to David (2 Samuel 19:18–20)

12 In His forbearance, God "crossed above" old sins (2 words) (Romans 3:25)

13 "Cancellation" of sins (Matthew 26:28)

15 Forgive others as God in _____ forgave you (Ephesians 4:32)

16 "Favored" is he whose sin is forgiven (Psalm 32:1)

20 The servant owing one hundred of these wasn't forgiven (Matthew 18:28)

21 The creditor forgave the "two who owed" him money (Luke 7:41–43)

22 He begged Moses and Aaron's forgiveness (Exodus 10:16–17)

24 If God's people repented, He would heal their _____ (2 Chronicles 7:14)

25 Peter told this sorcerer to repent (Acts 8:18–22)

27 It covers a multitude of sins (1 Peter 4:8)

36

*D*ecode one of the greatest statements in the Bible from the Great Shepherd to us, His sheep!

*Clue:* MESSIAH *is* EKGGUAL

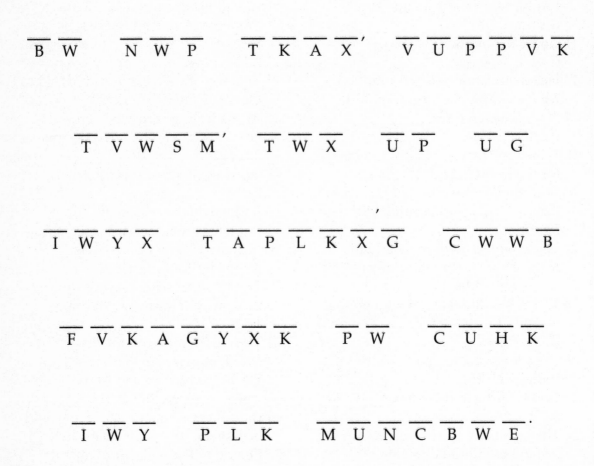

B W  N W P  T K A X,  V U P P V K

T V W S M,  T W X  U P  U G

I W Y X  T A P L K X G,  C W W B

F V K A G Y X K  P W  C U H K

I W Y  P L K  M U N C B W E.

When the bones were connected, they could walk around. Oh, hear the word of the Lord—as told in Ezekiel 37.

**Across**

5 Burial plots (v. 12)
7 Tranquility (v. 26)
8 Bones were dry, "optimism" was lost (v. 11)
10 The stick of Ephraim was in the hand of _____ (v. 16)
11 Abide (v. 25)
12 Royal leader (v. 22)
14 Registered nurse (abbr.)
15 Eternal (v. 26)
20 The son of #12 Across (v. 25)
22 Purify (v. 23)
23 Law (v. 24)

24 Rod (v. 16)

**Down**

1 Easy to hate (v. 23)
2 The people will have one "lamb leader" (v. 24)
3 God's servant, whose name means "supplanter" (v. 25)
4 Can these dead bones _____ ? Yes! (v. 3)
6 "I will be their God, and they shall be My _____ " (v. 27)
9 Republic (v. 22)
10 Ruling (v. 24)

11 Debase (v. 23)
13 The four winds breathed on the "killed" (v. 9)
14 Clattering (v. 7)
16 Tendons (v. 6)
17 Dale or dell (v. 1)
18 The dry bones hadn't drawn their last _____ , after all (v. 5)
19 The apple of God's eye (v. 24)
20 Postscript (abbr.)
21 The bones were the "family" of Israel (v. 11)

# DOWN TO EGYPT

"Get out of your country, from your family and from your father's house, to a land that I will show you" (Genesis 12:1).

So said God to Abram, and so began Abram's journey to Canaan.

But there was a famine in Canaan sometime after Abram and Sarai, his wife, arrived. Abram decided to pack up and move to Egypt, at least temporarily. That decision led to some trouble, but God kept all His promises to this future "father of a multitude."

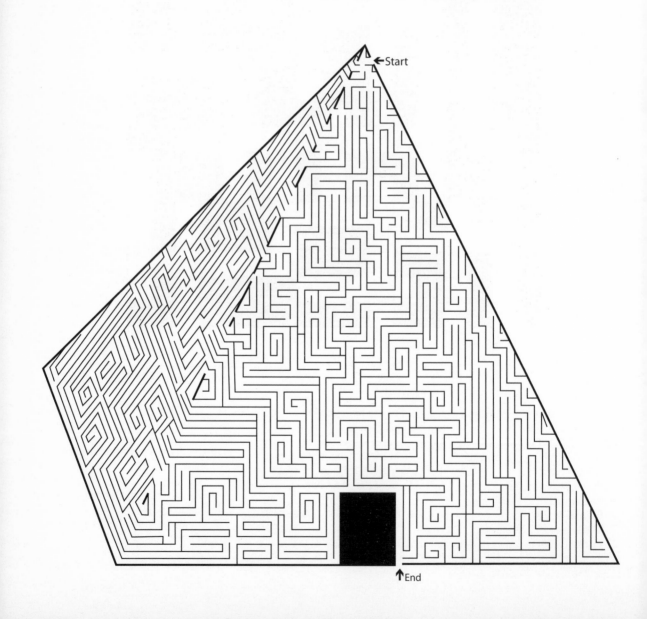

*U*se words reflecting prosperity from Deuteronomy 28:1–14 to complete the grid, and discover what they have in common from God's perspective.

Now it shall come to pass, if you diligently obey the voice of the Lord your God, to observe carefully all His commandments which I command you today, that the Lord your God will set you ____ above all nations of the earth. And all these blessings shall come upon you and overtake you, because you obey the voice of the Lord your God:

Blessed shall you be in the city, and blessed shall you be in the ____.

Blessed shall be the ____ of your body, the ____ of your ground and the increase of your ____, the increase of your ____ and the offspring of your ____.

Blessed shall be your basket and your kneading ____.

Blessed shall you be when you ____ in, and blessed shall you be when you ____ out.

The Lord will cause your ____ who rise against you to be defeated before your face; they shall come out against you one way and flee before you seven ways.

The Lord will command the blessing on you in your ____ and in all to which you set your hand, and He will bless you in the ____ which the Lord your God is giving you.

The Lord will ____ you as a holy people to Himself,

lust as He has sworn to you, if you keep the commandments of the Lord your God and walk in His ways. Then all peoples of the earth shall see that you are called by the name of the Lord, and they shall be afraid of you. And the Lord will grant you ____ of goods, in the fruit of your body, in the ____ of your livestock, and in the produce of your ground, in the land of which the Lord swore to your fathers to give you. The Lord will open to you His good ____, the heavens, to give the ____ to your land in its season, and to bless all the ____ of your hand. You shall ____ to many nations,

but you shall not borrow. And the Lord will make you the ____ and not the tail; you shall be ____ only, and not be beneath, if you heed the commandments of the Lord your God, which I command you today, and are careful to observe them. So you shall not turn aside from any of the words which I command you this day, to the right or the left, to go after other gods to serve them.

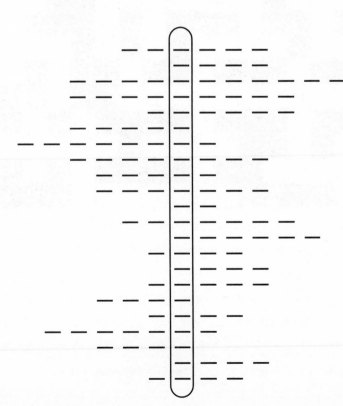

*T*he Bible has a great deal to say about learning, observing, studying, thinking, and meditating. Provide the missing words in the sixteen statements below to complete the crossword grid.

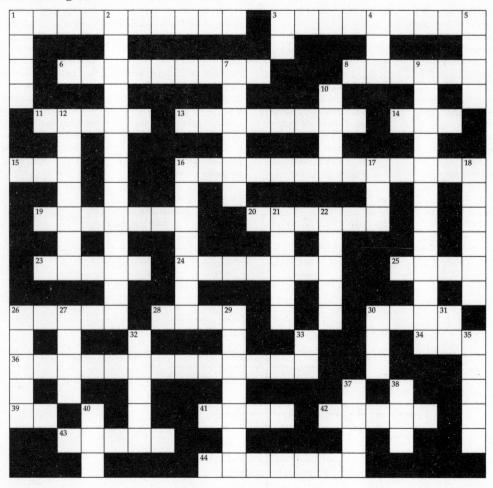

1 Take heed to yourself, and _____ keep yourself, lest you forget the things your _____ have seen, and lest they
          1 Across                                                       28 Across

   _____ from your heart all _____ days of your life. And teach them to your children and your _____
   8 Across                  4 Down                                                   2 Down
   (Deuteronomy 4:9)

2 The Lord said to His people in Horeb: "Gather the people to Me, and I will let them hear My _____ , that they may
                                                                                         11 Across

   learn to _____ Me all the days they live on the _____ , and that they may teach their children" (Deuteronomy 4:10)
   41 Across                             43 Across

3 Moses called all Israel, and said to them: "Hear, O Israel, the statutes and judgments which I speak in your hearing

   today, that you may learn them and be careful to _____ them" (Deuteronomy 5:1)
                                                     12 Down

4 He [the king] shall write for himself a copy of this _____ in a book, . . . and he shall read it all the days of his _____
      40 Down                                                                                                                          25 Across

, that he may learn to fear the LORD his God and be careful to observe all the words of this law and these statutes,

that his _____ may not be lifted above his brethren, that he may not turn aside from the commandment to the right
      32 Down

hand or to the left, and that he may _____ his _____ in his kingdom, he and his children in the midst of Israel
                                   19 Across   1 Down

(Deuteronomy 17:18–20)

5 I remember the days of _____ ; I meditate on all Your _____ ; I muse on the work of Your hands. I spread out my
                        38 Down                        26 Down

hands to _____ ; my soul longs for You like a thirsty land (Psalm 143:5–6)
        14 Across

6 Learn to _____ _____ ; seek justice, rebuke the oppressor; defend the fatherless, plead for the _____ (Isaiah 1:17)
     31 Down 37 Down                                                                                        35 Down

7 When you come into the land which the LORD your God is giving you, you shall not _____ to follow the _____ of
                                                                              23 Across              9 Down

those nations (Deuteronomy 18:9)

8 _____ the people together, _____ and _____ and little ones, and the stranger who is within your gates, that they
  18 Down                    30 Down    26 Across

may hear and that they may learn to fear the LORD your God and carefully observe all the words of this law

(Deuteronomy 31:12)

9 Give me _____ that I may learn Your commandments (Psalm 119:73)
         16 Across

10 _____ , by _____ spirit within me I will seek You early; for when Your judgments are in the earth, the inhabitants of
   15 Across   3 Down

the world will learn _____ (Isaiah 26:9)
                   36 Across

11 Blessed is the man who walks not in the counsel of the _____ , nor _____ in the path of _____ , _____ _____ in the
                                                      16 Down     7 Down              29 Down 17 Down 5 Down

_____ of the scornful; but his _____ is in the law of the LORD, and in His law he _____ day and _____ (Psalm
10 Down                        24 Across                                           3 Across        21 Down
1:1–2)

12 Let my heart be _____ regarding Your _____ , that I may not be _____ (Psalm 119:80)
                  6 Across              13 Across              44 Across

13 You shall love the LORD your God with all your heart, with all your soul, and with all your _____ (Matthew 22:37)
                                                                                        30 Across

14 The preparations of the heart belong to man, but the _____ of the tongue is from the LORD (Proverbs 16:1)
                                                    20 Across

15 What I say to you, I say to all: _____ ! (Mark 13:37)
                                22 Down

16 The wise men who came from the East to present gifts to the young child Jesus are also called _____
                                                                                            27 Down

17 _____ he thinks in his heart, _____ is he (Proverbs 23:7)
   33 Down                       39 Across

18 They _____ the wind, and reap the whirlwind (Hosea 8:7)
       34 Across

19 We know that we are of God, and the whole _____ lies under the sway of the wicked one. And we know that the
                                        42 Across

Son of God has come and has given us an understanding, that we may know Him who is true (1 John 5:19–20)

# $A$ll parts of this equation are from the book of Numbers—*naturally!*

The year after the children of Israel came out of Egypt and the Lord said to Moses, "Take a census of all the congregation" (Numbers 1:1–2)   $=$ _____

Multiplied by . . .
Number of tribes included in the census (Numbers 1:47)   $\times$ _____

Multiplied by . . .
Number of covered carts used to bring an offering to the Lord for the tabernacle (Numbers 7:3)   $\times$ _____

Multiplied by . . .
The worth in shekels of silver in the platter given to the Lord (Numbers 7:13)   $\times$ _____

Multiplied by . . .
The worth in shekels of the silver in the bowl given to the Lord (Numbers 7:13)   $\times$ _____

Divided by . . .
Number of silver trumpets made for calling the congregation and directing the movement of the camp (Numbers 10:2)   $\div$ _____

Plus . . .
The worth in shekels of the gold pan filled with incense given to the Lord (Numbers 7:14)   $=$ _____

Multiplied by . . .
The animals in the peace offerings (Numbers 7:17)

*Number of rams*   $\times$ _____

*Number of male goats*   $\times$ _____

*Number of male rams*   $\times$ _____

*Number of oxen*   $\times$ _____ $=$ $+$ _____

Plus . . .
The number of animals for the burnt offering (Numbers 7:87)

*Number of oxen*   $=$ _____

*Number of rams*   $+$ _____

*Number of male lambs*   $+$ _____

The number of kid goats for the sin offering (Numbers 7:87)   $+$ _____   $=$ _____

Multiplied by . . .
Number of days Miriam was shut out of the camp (Numbers 12:15)   $\times$ _____ $=$ $+$ _____

Plus . . .
"Retirement" age of levitical priest (Numbers 8:25)   $=$ _____

Multiplied by . . .
The number of turtle doves for an atonement offering for a Nazirite who touched a corpse (Numbers 6:10)   $\times$ _____ $=$ $+$ _____

Plus . . .
The day of the month of the celebration of Passover (Numbers 9:3)   $+$ _____

Equals . . .
The census of all "able to go to war" (from twenty years old and above) (Numbers 1:45–46)   $=$ _____

# THE EIGHT-POINTED STAR

*A* star with eight points has long been an emblem of baptism, since eight is the biblical number used to symbolize the regeneration of man.

Jesus was given His name at the time of His circumcision when He was eight days old, and a Christian child receives his name at baptism. In early instances of adult baptism, new believers frequently changed their names at the time they were baptized. The changing of the name added to the symbolism of regeneration in baptism. In many churches, the base of the baptismal font is octagonal, or eight-sided.

The fact that eight souls were saved in the ark—Noah and his wife, and their three sons and their wives—has been associated with the symbol. The appearance of a new star in the sky at the time of Jesus' birth is also linked to the symbolism of the eight-point star.

Start →

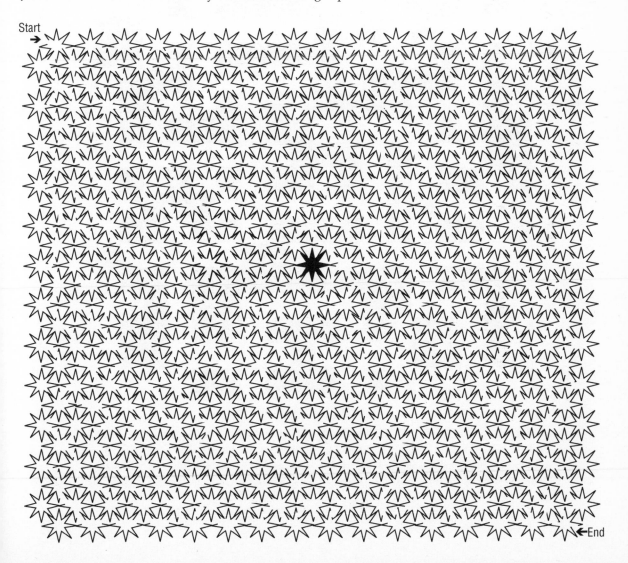

←End

43

This crossword is based on the words of Martin Luther's famous hymn, "A Mighty Fortress." See how much of the puzzle you can complete before consulting the Word Pool.

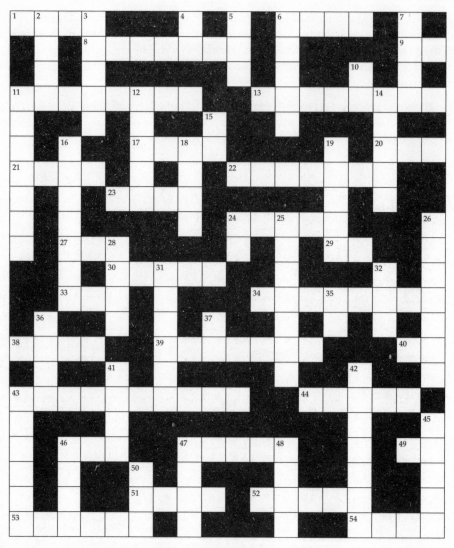

## Word Pool

ABIDETH AGE ALSO AMID ARMED BE BULWARK CRUEL DOOM DOST
EARTH EARTHLY ENDURE EQUAL FAILING FEAR FORTRESS GIFTS GO
GOODS GREAT GRIM HE HIM ILLS IS IT KILL KINDRED KINGDOM LO
LORD MAN MORTAL MUST NAME ON ONE OURS POWER PREVAILING
PRINCE RAGE SAME SEEK STILL STRENGTH STRIVING THO TO TREMBLE
TRIUMPH TRUTH UNDO US WE WIN WOE WORD WORLD

**1.**

A mighty _____ is our God,
         (11 Across)

A _____ never _____;
 (42 Down)        (11 Down)

Our Helper He, _____ the flood
                (46 Down)

Of mortal _____ _____.
          (23 Across) (43 Across)

For _____ our ancient foe
    (45 Down)

Doth _____ to work us _____;
     (38 Across)            (50 Down)

His craft and _____ are _____,
              (52 Across)    (24 Across)

And _____ with _____ hate,
    (30 Across)     (44 Across)

On _____ is not His _____.
   (3 Down)              (12 Down)

**2.**

Did we in our own _____ confide,
                  (13 Across)

Our _____ would be losing,
    (34 Across)

Were not the right Man _____ our side,
                       (10 Down)

The _____ of God's own choosing.
    (27 Across)

_____ ask who that may _____?
(18 Down)                   (37 Down)

Christ Jesus, _____ _____ _____;
              (49 Across) (35 Down) (29 Across)

_____ Sabaoth, His _____,
(21 Across)            (28 Down)

From age to _____ the _____,
            (46 Across)    (41 Down)

And He _____ _____ the battle.
       (7 Down)   (32 Down)

**3.**

And _____ this _____, with devils filled,
    (5 Down)       (47 Across)

Should threaten to _____ us,
                   (17 Across)

We will not _____, for God hath willed
            (36 Down)

His truth to _____ through us.
             (16 Down)

The _____ of Darkness _____,
    (43 Down)              (6 Across)

We _____ not for him;
   (39 Across)

His _____ _____ can _____,
    (1 Across) (4 Down)      (53 Across)

For _____, his _____ is sure;
    (40 Across)     (48 Down)

_____ little word shall fell _____.
(20 Across)                      (33 Across)

**4.**

That _____ above all _____ powers,
     (47 Down)            (25 Down)

No thanks _____ them, _____;
          (15 Down)       (8 Across)

The Spirit and the _____ are _____
                   (6 Down)      (51 Across)

Thru him who with _____ sideth.
                  (9 Across)

Let _____ and _____ _____,
    (14 Down)     (22 Across) (24 Down)

This _____ life _____;
     (31 Down)       (2 Down)

The body they may _____;
                  (54 Across)

God's _____ abideth still;
      (19 Down)

His _____ is forever.
    (26 Down)

*U*se the missing words of Deuteronomy 28:20–30 to complete the grid, and discover an important consequence of behavior.

The Lord will send on you cursing, ____, and ____ in all that you set your hand to do, until you are ____ and until you ____ quickly, because of the wickedness of your doings in which you have forsaken Me. The Lord will make the ____ cling to you until He has consumed you from the land which you are going to possess. The Lord will strike you with ____, with ____,

with ____, with severe burning fever, with the ____, with ____, and with ____; they shall pursue you until you perish. And your heavens which are over your head shall be bronze, and the earth which is under you shall be iron. The Lord will change the rain of your land to powder and ____; from the heaven it shall come down on you until you are destroyed.

The Lord will cause

you to be ____ before your enemies; you shall go out one way against them and flee seven ways before them; and you shall become ____ to all the kingdoms of the earth. Your carcasses shall be food for all the birds of the air and the beasts of the earth, and no one shall frighten them away. The Lord will strike you with the ____ of Egypt, with ____, with the ____, and with

the ____, from which you cannot be healed. The Lord will strike you with ____ and ____ and confusion of heart. And you shall grope at noonday, as a blind man gropes in darkness; you shall not prosper in your ways; you shall be only ____ and ____ continually, and no one shall save you.

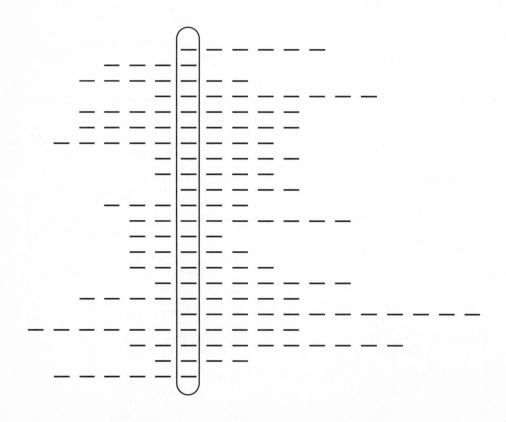

# TO THE TOMB

*H*ave you ever opened a box, hoping to find a special surprise inside—only to discover that the box was empty?

Sometimes empty is good. When we "empty" our lives into God's hands, He can use us to bring others to Him.

When Peter ran to Jesus' tomb on the third day after His crucifixion, finding it empty was wonderful! Jesus had risen from the dead, just as He said He would!

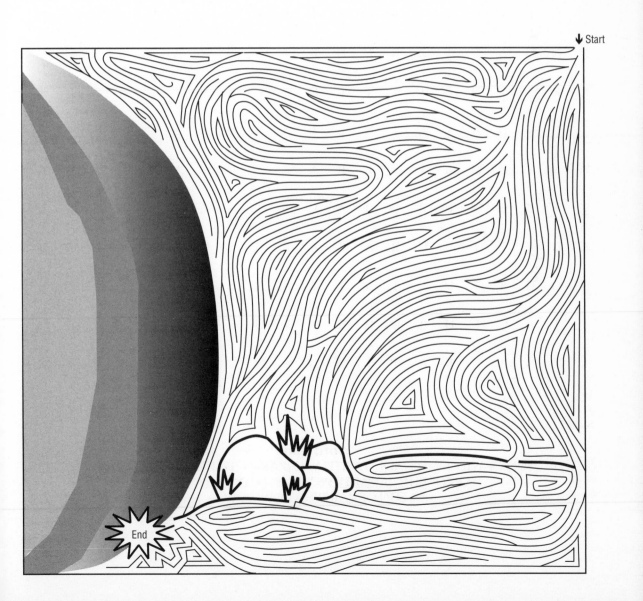

*I*n the letter box below are the words that relate to eight people in the Bible who died and were resurrected and restored to life. See if you can find them in five minutes or less!

```
A B C D A U R J A H N A Z A R D E F O P Q

G H I P S G R A H T I B A T U R S T U V W

J K L I H Z A A H A I B A T S J A I R S N

M N O A U T Z R U H B I S H U A I N S H U

O R S T N E J N J P R L U S N T U V E U T

T U V S A N A I N E I A S N A Y C H U S Z

W X Y H M A I S E R A Z E R M A R E P H A

Z A B U M L R U S A L J J A Z T H J E S U

C D E T I S U R A Z A L S I U L A Z A R U

F G H Y T U S I A J I A N E S N A I T A B

I J K C E H S U H C Y T U E J I T H A D O

L M N A L B A T I M M A N S E R C A S E U
```

**Word Pool**
SON OF WIDOW IN <u>NAIN</u>   TABITHA   LAZARUS   DAUGHTER OF <u>JAIRUS</u>
SON OF <u>SHUNAMMITE</u> WOMAN   EUTYCHUS   JESUS
SON OF <u>ZAREPHATH</u> WIDOW

*W*hen it comes to "figurin'"—these words from the Bible are worth rememberin'!

## *Clue:* MESSIAH *is* GYMMCUB

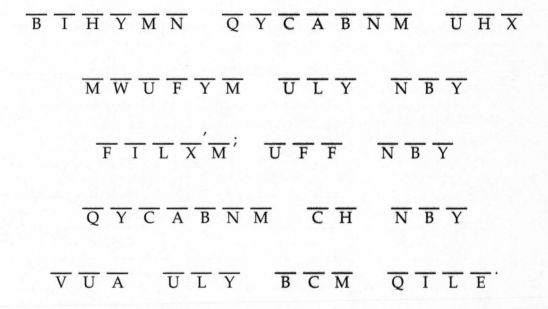

B I H Y M N  Q Y C A B N M  U H X

M W U F Y M  U L Y  N B Y

F I L X M';  U F F  N B Y

Q Y C A B N M  C H  N B Y

V U A  U L Y  B C M  Q I L E.

# CORNELIUS'S PLEA

*R*oman soldiers were not given to having visions. But Cornelius, a Gentile and a member of the Italian Regiment, was devout.

In a vision, God told him to send men to Joppa to find Simon Peter, saying, "He will tell you what you must do" (Acts 10:6).

The next day, Peter saw a vision of his own. The message: the gospel is for Jews *and* Gentiles. Therefore, when Cornelius's men arrived, Peter was ready to go with them.

Cornelius's servants must spell Simon Peter's name, in correct letter order. Do not cross back over a path that you have already used.

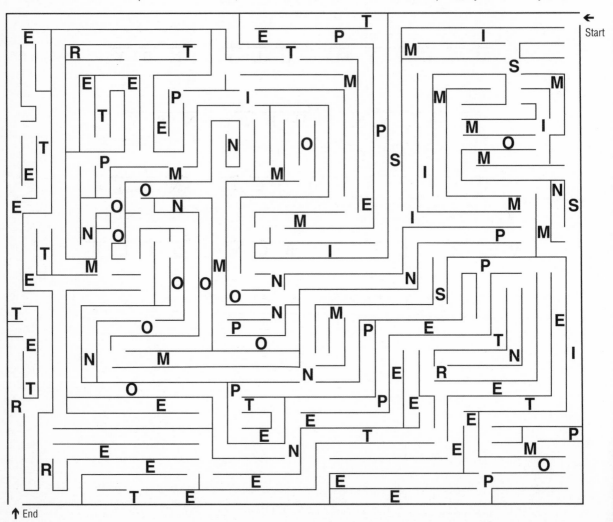

*J*ehoshaphat got the jump on his enemies, thanks to God's intervention. This puzzle about the king is from 2 Chronicles 20.

## Across

6 Enemies came up by this "rise" (3 words) (v. 16)
8 Jehoshaphat was king of ____ (v. 35)
9 Jehoshaphat's mother (v. 31)
12 Disaster by "blade" (v. 9)
13 Afterwards, the people gathered in this valley (v. 26)
17 It took ____ days to gather spoils (v. 25)
19 His age when his reign ended (v. 31)
22 They never made it to Tarshish (v. 37)
23 A temple for God (v. 8)

## Down

1 Enemies were near the Wilderness of ____ (v. 16)
2 His realm was "peaceful" afterwards (v. 30)
3 Son of Zechariah (v. 14)
4 The people of Judah went into this wilderness (v. 20)
5 Jehoshaphat "lowered" his head (v. 18)
7 Hazazon Tamar, which is ____ ____ (2 words) (v. 2)
10 Praise the "grace" of holiness (v. 21)
11 Ammon and Moab killed inhabitants of ____ ____ (2 words) (v. 23)

12 God will "rescue" (v. 9)
14 Stringed instrument (v. 28)
15 He proclaimed one (v. 3)
16 The Lord set them (sing.) (v. 22)
18 The battle was His (poss.) (v. 15)
20 They returned to Jerusalem with "gladness" (v. 27)
21 His father (v. 32)

Find fifteen things that the Bible describes as hiding out in caves, dens, and lairs.

```
V  A  E  R  G  I  K  O  D  I  S  N  M  M  O  C
I  Y  O  U  N  S  L  A  K  C  A  J  A  P  E  R
E  O  L  G  I  D  E  N  S  M  O  B  N  I  R  G
V  I  P  E  R  S  N  R  E  R  C  D  A  V  R  S
E  N  S  I  M  M  S  E  L  M  S  E  S  E  D  E
R  O  D  G  O  A  R  R  I  E  Y  R  A  C  E  V
Y  R  T  L  C  F  E  Y  O  D  N  T  N  O  M  A
S  E  H  S  Y  L  D  O  M  O  M  L  H  A  M  L
L  A  I  R  S  O  N  U  N  E  G  I  M  G  V  K
A  T  E  I  D  Y  A  L  N  S  V  O  H  T  I  S
V  V  V  L  K  O  M  I  O  E  A  E  I  N  G  M
E  S  E  A  I  U  M  N  J  S  K  L  G  M  E  N
M  B  S  N  G  N  O  S  A  C  S  S  E  M  R  O
I  E  T  S  R  I  C  H  M  E  N  N  R  A  S  M
G  T  L  A  D  T  E  R  E  V  O  S  M  N  V  C
H  Y  V  O  S  M  O  G  S  I  I  O  I  D  A  I
R  I  L  C  H  T  N  T  L  H  L  N  T  X  R  R
M  S  M  R  Q  U  S  H  I  T  G  N  O  B  I  O
J  T  A  C  R  A  J  A  C  K  N  D  C  E  P  R
N  A  S  O  A  R  B  O  E  B  U  E  S  R  N  T
A  I  C  B  M  A  S  A  R  B  O  C  K  A  L  S
L  S  O  K  M  V  I  J  A  G  Y  R  S  Y  O  U
```

**Scripture Pool**
JOB 37:8    PSALM 10:9; 104:21    ISAIAH 2:18–19; 11:8
JEREMIAH 7:11; 10:22    REVELATION 6:15–17

# ALPHA AND OMEGA

*A*lpha is the first letter of the Greek alphabet, Omega the last letter.

Three times in the book of Revelation, the phrase is used. The first time, in Revelation 1:8, God the Father spoke: "I am the Alpha and the Omega, the Beginning and the End . . . who is and who was and who is to come, the Almighty."

In Revelation 21:6 and 22:13, Jesus was the one speaking: "I am the Alpha and the Omega, the Beginning and the End" and, "I am the Alpha and Omega, the Beginning and the End, the First and the Last."

The threefold use of the phrase underscores its importance.

The phrase points to Christ as being both the source and the sum of everything—the Creator and the Culminator.

Start →

←End

*T*he ark of the covenant had been away from home for too long, so King David decided it was time to bring it back to Jerusalem—which he did—after a couple of interruptions. The answers to this crossword are found in 1 Chronicles 13–16.

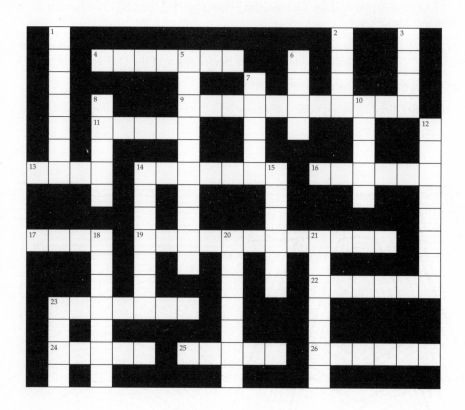

## Across

4 Only they could carry the ark (15:2)
9 Where David defeated the Philistines (2 words) (14:10–11)
11 Burnt offerings and ____ offerings (16:2)
13 One of two who drove the cart (13:7)
14 Ask advice (15:13)
16 #14 Down's material (15:19)
17 "Look for" the Lord (16:11)
19 The animals that were sacrificed (3 words) (15:26)
22 The ark's previous location was #18 Down ____ (13:5)
23 Grandeur (16:27)
24 Sacrifices were put on this (16:40)
25 The ark was at the Gittite's house for ____ months (13:13-14)
26 The threshing floor's owner (13:9)

## Down

1 One of the ark's doorkeepers (15:23)
2 The other cart driver (13:7)
3 Obed-____ was the Gittite in #25 Across (13:14)
5 David built this home for the ark (16:1)
6 They pulled the cart (13:9)
7 A Levite who helped carry the ark (15:11–12)
8 David wore this linen garment (15:27)
10 One of two priests who helped carry the ark (15:11–12)
12 God dwelt between these two winged creatures on the lid of the ark (13:6)
14 With clashing ____, they made music (13:8)
15 Gratitude (16:8)
18 The ark's previous location ____ #22 Across (13:5)
20 Vocal music makers (15:16)
21 Exult (16:31)
23 David gave all Israelites a loaf of bread, a piece of "flesh," and a raisin cake when the ark returned (16:3)

$D$ecode the message below to find one of the most famous statements from the book of Job.

### Clue: MESSIAH *is* ZNVVDOQ

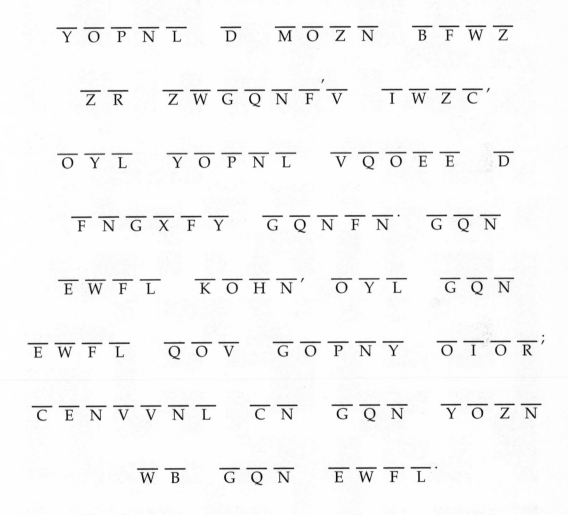

Y O P N L    D    M O Z N    B F W Z

Z R    Z W G Q N F V '    I W Z C '

O Y L    Y O P N L    V Q O E E    D

F N G X F Y    G Q N F N    G Q N

E W F L    K O H N '    O Y L    G Q N

E W F L    Q O V    G O P N Y    O I O R ;

C E N V V N L    C N    G Q N    Y O Z N

W B    G Q N    E W F L .

*A*ll of the clues in the "D-vine," difficult, daring crossword below begin with the letter *D*.

## Across

3 Pious

5 Victor over Goliath (1 Samuel 17)

7 Jesus gave His disciples power to heal "all kinds of ____" (Matthew 10:1)

8 Finished

10 Paul said Jesus "will judge the living and the ____" (2 Timothy 4:1)

11 Marked by lies and twisted information

12 The prophet Haggai called the Messiah "the ____ of All Nations" (Haggai 2:7)

15 "The LORD of hosts will ____ them," says Zechariah 9:15

17 Said Paul of Jesus, "Death no longer has ____ over Him" (Romans 6:9)

19 Goddess of Ephesus, whose temple Paul challenged (Acts 19:28–34)

20 Saul met the LORD on the road to this city (Acts 9:1–6)

22 Jesus taught, "A ____ is not above his teacher" (Matthew 10:24)

23 Old English for refuse; anything nauseating or loathsome

24 The king who, against his own personal convictions, had Daniel thrown to the lions (Daniel 6)

25 Demon

26 Jesus accused the money changers of turning the house of prayer into a "____ of thieves" (Matthew 21:13)

27 Paul wrote to Timothy, "Let everyone who names the name of Christ ____ from iniquity" (2 Timothy 2:19)

30 Leah's daughter (Genesis 30:20–21)

31 "Your sons and your ____ shall prophesy" says Joel 2:28

32 Jesus told a parable in which a rich man cried for Lazarus to ____ the tip of his finger in water and touch his parched tongue (Luke 16:24)

34 Goliath called, "I ____ the armies of Israel this day" (1 Samuel 17:10)

35 "____ me speedily" is the psalmist's cry in Psalm 31:2

36 Jesus said, "If anyone desires to come after Me, let him ____ himself, and take up his cross, and follow Me" (Matthew 16:24)

38 Job repented in "____ and ashes" (Job 42:6)

39 Prison; Joseph was called out of this place by Pharaoh (Genesis 41:14)

40 Joseph had a God-given ability to interpret them (Genesis 40–41)

41 Edomite who killed eighty-five priests upon King Saul's order after David's escape (1 Samuel 22:18)

42 Paul commended the Jews in Berea because they "searched the Scriptures ____" (Acts 17:11)

46 The Lord said, "I knew you in the wilderness, in the land of great ____" (Hosea 13:5)

47 Jesus taught, "Observe and ____" (Matthew 23:3)

49 The Lord holds the rulers of the earth who plot against Him "In ____ ," says Psalm 2:4

51 The Bible says of Noah: "According to all that God commanded him, so he ____" (Genesis 6:22)

52 Paul sent for Timothy, in part, because Titus had departed for ____ (2 Timothy 4:9–10)

53 The ability to correctly see and understand the difference between right and wrong, good and evil

54 Jeweled turban, in Old English

55 "Better is a ____ of herbs where love is, than a fatted calf with hatred" (Proverbs 15:17)

56 "Keep your heart with all ____, for out of it spring the issues of life" (Proverbs 4:23)

57 Fruit of a palm tree in the Middle East

## Down

1 After His baptism, Jesus saw "the Spirit of God descending like a ____ and alighting upon Him" (Matthew 3:16)

2 The state of a human being who touches uncleanness (Leviticus 5:3)

3 When the ark of the covenant was brought into Jerusalem, David "____ before the LORD with all his might" (2 Samuel 6:14)

4 He abandoned Paul "having loved this present world" (2 Timothy 4:10)

5 Silversmith who led a revolt against Paul (Acts 19:24–27)

6 The means by which Paul tells Titus to "exhort and convict those who contradict" (Titus 1:9)

7 An "office" in the early church (1 Timothy 3:10)

9 Paul warned the Colossians against those who would "cheat you through philosophy and empty ____" (Colossians 2:8)

10 Jesus healed a man with this condition by putting His fingers in his ears (Mark 7:32–35)

13 Also called Tabitha, Peter raised her from the dead (Acts 9:36–41)

14 Jesus taught, "Every city or house ____ against itself will not stand" (Matthew 12:25)

15 He was thrown into a den of lions (Daniel 6:16)

16 A woman believer in Athens (Acts 17:34)

18 She helped Barak lead the Israelites into battle against Sisera (Judges 4:4–16)

20 Ceremony of commitment to the Lord (Nehemiah 12:27)

21 Divinely ordained future; role in the kingdom of God

23 Modern for "thou shalt not" (2 words)

26 Philistine god, whose image fell in presence of the ark (1 Samuel 5:1–5)

27 He who hates his brother "is in ____ ," according to 1 John 2:9

28 To eat together

29 "The evening and the morning were the first ____" (Genesis 1:5)

32 "Make known His ____ among the peoples!" declares Psalm 105:1

33 Samson's downfall (Judges 16:4–21)

35 Ehud's weapon, used to kill Eglon (Judges 3:16)

37 A waterless place

38 Jesus taught, "If you have faith and do not ____" you will receive whatever things you ask in prayer (Matthew 21:21–22)

40 Elijah and Elisha crossed the Jordan on ____ ground (2 Kings 2:8)

41 Rhoda forgot to open it in her excitement at hearing Peter's voice (Acts 12:13–16)

43 Plain on which golden image of Nebuchadnezzar was set up (Daniel 3:1)

44 Peter admonished, "Be ____ to be found by Him in peace, without spot and blameless" (2 Peter 3:14)

45 "Let them praise His name with the ____ ,"says Psalm 149:3

47 The psalmist's soul panted for God like the "____ pants for the water brooks" (Psalm 42:1)

48 Gives up life

50 Supped and eaten

51 To reside

52 One of Noah's great-great-grandsons (Genesis 10:1.6–7)

53 Bilhah's son, one of the twelve tribes of Israel (Genesis 35:25)

54 "Blessed are the dead who ____ in the Lord" (Revelation 14:13)

The number seven in the Bible is the number of completion and perfection. In the letter box below are hidden seventeen words from the book of Revelation that are associated with the number seven. After you have circled all the hidden words, read the remaining words to find the promise found in Revelation 3:5–6.

| | | | | | | | | | | | | | |
|---|---|---|---|---|---|---|---|---|---|---|---|---|---|
| H | E | W | H | O | O | V | E | R | C | O | S | M | E | S | S |
| H | A | S | E | Y | E | L | L | B | E | S | C | L | L | O | T |
| H | E | R | D | I | N | W | H | I | N | T | E | A | A | G | A |
| R | M | E | E | S | E | H | C | R | U | H | C | M | N | E | T |
| S | A | D | N | D | I | W | O | I | L | L | N | P | O | T | S |
| B | L | N | O | S | T | H | O | U | T | H | I | S | S | N | A |
| T | R | U | M | P | E | T | S | M | E | F | M | T | R | O | M |
| T | H | H | E | A | B | U | O | O | K | E | O | A | F | L | I |
| F | E | T | D | B | U | T | G | I | D | W | I | N | L | L | C |
| O | N | S | F | E | S | S | K | A | S | H | I | D | S | N | A |
| M | E | P | B | T | L | E | I | F | L | S | S | S | O | R | E |
| M | Y | I | A | F | E | D | N | A | T | P | H | L | E | R | A |
| N | D | R | B | E | G | F | G | O | R | M | E | H | W | I | S |
| A | S | I | N | G | N | E | S | N | I | A | T | N | U | O | M |
| L | S | T | H | E | A | W | H | O | H | L | A | S | A | N | B |
| E | A | S | R | L | E | T | H | I | M | H | E | A | R | W | H |
| A | T | T | H | E | S | P | I | R | I | T | S | A | Y | S | . |

**Word Pool**

ANGELS  BOWLS  CHURCHES  DIADEMS  EYES  HEADS  HORNS  KINGS
LAMPS  LAMPSTANDS  MOUNTAINS  PLAGUES  SEALS  SPIRITS  STARS
THUNDERS  TRUMPETS

# TO THE CATHEDRAL

We were created to have a personal relationship with God and to worship Him. Private Bible study and prayer are essential to our fellowship with God, but we also need to meet with other believers on a regular basis.

Hebrew 10:24–25 says, "And let us consider one another in order to stir up love and good works, not forsaking the assembling of ourselves together."

One voice can praise God, but how beautiful is the harmony of sopranos, altos, tenors, and basses.

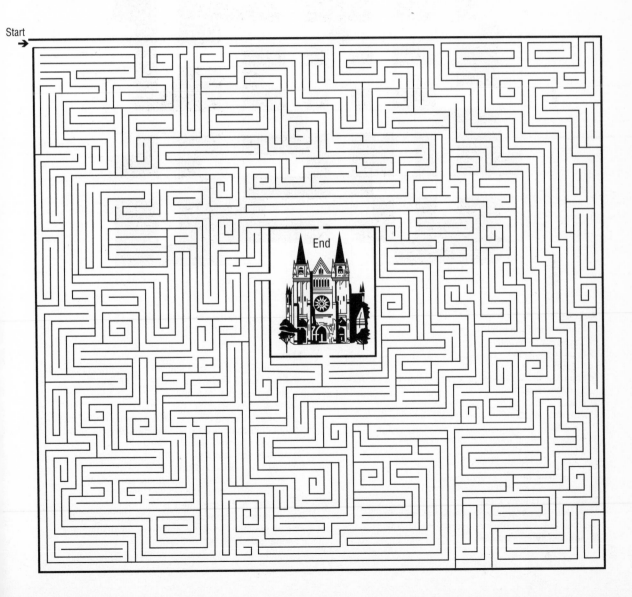

*W*hatever form suffering takes in our lives, it's comforting to know that Jesus was no stranger to it, either. And because He endured to the end, so can we.

## Across

3 Forbearance (James 5:10)
5 Deserving (Acts 5:41)
7 Postscript (abbr.)
8 Ill (James 5:14)
10 Some Galileans' blood was "mixed" with their sacrifices by Pilate (Luke 13:1)
11 Like
12 This church will suffer ten days of tribulation (Revelation 2:8, 10)
13 Woman with a flow of ____ (Mark 5:25–26)
17 Inactive (Proverbs 19:15)
18 Compliance (Hebrews 5:8)
19 For nothing, or in ____ (Galatians 3:4)
20 Take down a notch (Deuteronomy 8:2)
22 Intimidate (1 Peter 2:23)
25 Christ suffered for us in the "body" (1 Peter 4:1–2)
26 His sickness was for God's glory (John 11:2–4)
27 Anguish (Revelation 21:4)
28 Paul's ____ in the side (2 Corinthians 12:7–10)
29 Upbraid (1 Timothy 4:10)

## Down

1 Take up your ____, and follow Him (Matthew 16:24–25)
2 After testing, we become pure ____ (Job 23:10)
4 Strife (Philippians 1:30)
6 Lured (Hebrews 2:18)
7 Jesus ate this last meal with His disciples (Luke 22:15)
8 The Philistines took his sight (Judges 16:20–21)
9 We suffer for the "realm" of God (2 Thessalonians 1:5)
14 Anxiety (Romans 8:35)
15 Be plentiful (2 Corinthians 1:5)
16 "The ____ of His sufferings" (Philippians 3:10)
21 The just suffered for the ____ (1 Peter 3:18)
23 Tribulations (1 Peter 1:6)
24 "Is anyone . . . suffering? Let him ____" (James 5:13)
26 Paul gladly suffered the "forfeiture" of all things for Jesus' sake (Philippians 3:8)

Complete the message below to discover what is said in the wake of the opening of the sixth seal, and its resulting great earthquake, in the book of Revelation.

### *Clue:* MESSIAH *is* AIUUEMF

The kings of the earth, the great men, the rich men, the commanders, the mighty men, every slave and every free man, hid themselves in the caves and in the rocks of the mountains, and said to the mountains and rocks,

"
FALL  ON  US  AND
H M B B   Y Z   S U   M Z J

HIDE  US  FROM  THE
F E J I   S U   H V Y A   T F I

FACE  OF  HIM  WHO
H M K I   Y H   F E A   Q F Y

SITS  ON  THE  THRONE
U E T U   Y Z   T F I   T F V Y Z I

AND  FROM  THE  WRATH
M Z J   H V Y A   T F I   Q V M T F

OF  THE  LAMB!  FOR
Y H   T F I   B M A L   H Y V

THE  GREAT  DAY  OF
T F I   G V I M T   J M O   Y H

HIS  WRATH  HAS  COME'
F E U   Q V M T F   F M U   K Y A I

AND  WHO  IS  ABLE  TO
M Z J   Q F Y   E U   M L B I   T Y

STAND?"
U T M Z J

*O*ne of the most beloved and frequently memorized psalms is Psalm 23. See how many of the words you can supply for the grid below without looking up this passage in the Bible.

The LORD is my shepherd; I shall not want. He (3) me to (25) (19) in (6) (12); He leads me beside the (20) (29). He (9) my soul; He (7) me in the (1) of (2) for (16) (23) sake.

Yea, (22) I (4) through the (30) of the (5) of (17), I will fear no (24); for You are (8) me; Your (27) and Your (28), they (10) me.

You (15) a (32) before me in the presence of my (14); You (26) my head with oil; My cup (18) over. (21) (31) and (11) shall follow me all the days of my life; and I will dwell in the (13) of the LORD forever.

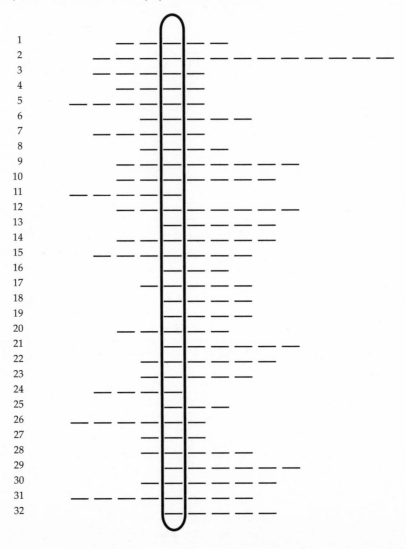

# Racing the Storm

Elijah knew the power of God. So he wasn't surprised when God sent fire from heaven to consume a burnt sacrifice that had been soaked with water (1 Kings 18:30–38).

In the third year of a drought, he knew he could tell King Ahab that the rain was about to come (1 Kings 18:41).

And when the rain came, do you think Elijah was surprised that God helped him outrun the downpour—and Ahab's chariot—to the entrance of Jezreel?

Start

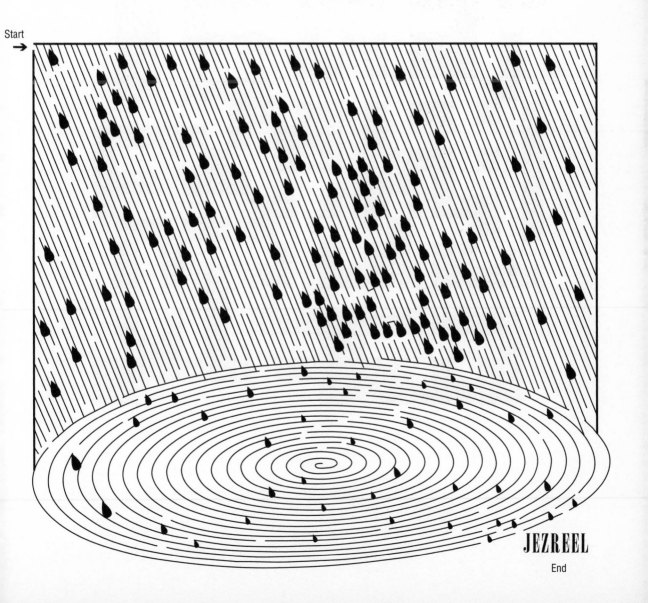

JEZREEL

End

*M*any Bible scholars believe that Colossians 1:15–20 is a hymn of the early church. Complete the words to this passage to complete the crossword. We've provided a Word Pool to help you.

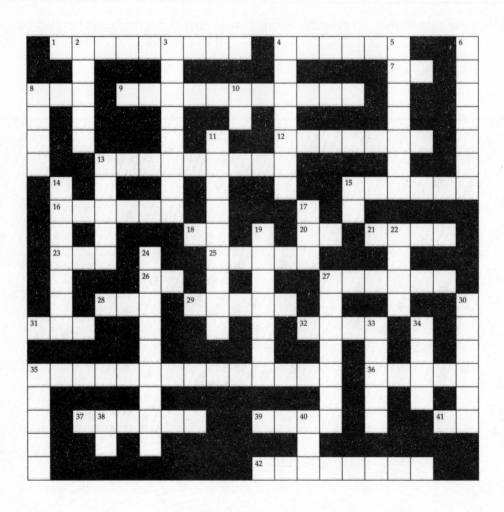

He is the _____ of the _____ _____, the _____ _____ all _____. For
    (13 Down)         (13 Across)(17 Down)    (11 Down)(22 Down)    (3 Down)

_____ _____ all _____ _____ created that _____ in heaven and that are on _____,
(15 Down)(28 Across)   (37 Across) (34 Down)       (31 Across)                    (2 Down)

_____and invisible, whether _____ or _____ or _____ _____ _____. All things were
(6 Down)                (12 Across)   (24 Down)  (35 Across) (41 Across) (27 Across)

_____ through Him and _____ Him. And _____ is _____ all things, and _____ Him all
(4 Down)           (8 Across)       (38 Down)  (15 Across)        (7 Across)

things _____. And He_____ the _____ of the _____, the _____, who is the beginning,
(19 Down)      (10 Down)   (32 Across)    (21 Across)   (4 Across)

the firstborn _____ the _____, that in _____ things He may have the _____. For _____
        (8 Down)   (39 Across)   (40 Down)             (9 Across)    (18 Across)

_____ the _____ that in Him all _____ _____ should _____, and by Him to _____
(27 Down)  (30 Down)         (23 Across) (42 Across)   (33 Down)       (1 Across)

all thing to _____, by Him, _____ things _____ _____ or things in _____ , having made
     (5 Down)       (14 Down)   (20 Across) (36 Across)     (16 Across)

_____ through the _____ _____ His _____ .
(35 Down)    (25 Across) (26 Across)  (29 Across)

## Word Pool

ALL   ARE   BEFORE   BLOOD   BODY   BY   CHURCH   CONSIST   CREATED
CREATION   CROSS   DEAD   DOMINIONS   DWELL   EARTH   EARTH
FATHER   FIRSTBORN   FOR   FROM   FULLNESS   GOD   HE   HEAD
HEAVEN   HIM   HIMSELF   IMAGE   IN   INVISIBLE   IS   IT   OF   ON   OR
OVER   PEACE   PLEASED   POWERS   PREEMINENCE   PRINCIPALITIES
RECONCILE   THE   THINGS   THRONES   VISIBLE   WERE   WHETHER

*(Duplicate words are intentional.)*

Complete the titles of these eleven famous Christmas songs to discover one of the most famous descriptions of Christmas Eve.

1 "Good _____ Men, Rejoice"

2 "O Come, All Ye _____"

3 "Joy to the _____"

4 "Hark! The Herald _____ Sing"

5 "O _____ _____" (2 words)

6 "We _____ King of Orient Are"

7 "It Came Upon a _____ Clear"

8 "The _____ Drummer Boy"

9 "Away in a _____"

10 "O Little Town of _____"

11 "The _____ Noel"

1 — — — — — — —

2 — — — — — — —

3 — — — — —

4 — — — — —

5 — — — — — — — —

6 — — — — —

7 — — — — — —

8 — — — — — —

9 — — — — — —

10 — — — — — — —

11 — — — — —

*F*ind fifteen words in the letter box below that relate to "heavenly beings." See how many you can find before consulting the Word Pool below.

```
M A N G A R R C H A E M E S S E N W O R
N I T H R E N G E L T N C I M G N I W S
I G N T F O A H M I D W O R S H I P O H
W M S I N E A C R I G I H R L E A H M I
H I C D S M N I A L H N A L H U C I C P
P U B I N T G C H A E P E E F T I E R T
L A I N I A E L E I R B A G T S H I D I
E R M G S M L R G M O V T R H H R P I M
G E S S T L B A I B E S O H E E A O E N
N H A E R E R C O N R E S Y L S V S W G
A C R I N I H L L C G A P H N E S M M S
H S E S G A N Y E H L S H I M E R I H C
C T R V E E H V N M E G P T N E B P H M
R N A L V O A Y L C I N R I S U I E N I
A T E H S E H G A B R I H C R B R I M N
M H A T O H O R H T E W E E O I T S I G
E O I R W R S N E L N O H A B R T E R S
S P H S E M F I C U E C N I R P A S V E
S E N G R E G N E S S E M H T S T N S R
```

**Word Pool**

SERAPHIM   HEAVENLY HOST   LUCIFER   MICHAEL   CHERUBIM   PRINCE
ARCHANGEL   GABRIEL   WINGS   TIDINGS   MINISTERING SPIRITS   ANGEL
THRONE   MESSENGER   WORSHIP

Complete the words to Isaiah 45:18–25—an "autobiography of the Almighty"—to work this crossword.

For thus says the LORD, Who _____ the _____, Who _____ _____, Who _____ the earth
            (14 Across)     (46 Across)     (37 Across) (35 Across)   (2 Down)

and made it, Who has_____ it, Who did not _____ it in vain, Who formed it to be_____ :
           (11 Down)        (55 Across)           (28 Across)

"_____ _____(2 words) the LORD, and there is no other. I have not spoken in _____, in a _____
  (36 Across)                                     (9 Down)   (50 Across)

place of the earth; I did not _____ to the _____of Jacob, '_____ _____ in vain'; I, the LORD,
                  (38 Down)    (9 Across)     (45 Down) (12 Across)

speak righteousness, I declare things that are _____.
                               (3 Down)

"_____ yourselves and come; draw_____ _____, you who have _____ from the nations. They
  (20 Across)              (53 Down) (32 Across)        (44 Down)

_____ no knowledge, _____ _____ the _____ of their carved _____, and _____ to a
(33 Down)             (22 Down) (27 Down)   (26 Down)       (10 Across)    (34 Across)

god that cannot _____. Tell and _____ forth your _____; yes, let them take _____ together.
          (16 Down)    (24 Across)      (13 Across)       (23 Across)

Who has _____this from _____ _____ (2 words)? Who has _____ it from that time? Have not I,
   (18 Down)        (40 Across)              (49 Across)

the LORD? And there is _____ _____God _____ Me, a _____ God and a _____; there is
            (19 Across) (52 Down)   (29 Down)    (21 Across)     (6 Across)

_____besides Me.
(5 Across)

"Look to Me, and _____ saved, all _____ _____ of the _____! For I am God, and there is no
       (8 Down)      (48 Across) (59 Across)   (56 Across)

other. I have sworn by _____; the _____ has _____out of My mouth in _____ , and shall not
          (42 Down)   (58 Across)  (4 Across)       (7 Down)

_____, that to Me every _____ shall _____, every _____ shall _____ _____ (2 words)
(43 Down)        (1 Down)   (25 Across)    (15 Down)    (49 Down)

oath. He shall say, 'Surely in the _____ I have righteousness and _____. To Him _____
              (31 Down)           (39 Down)    (17 Across)

shall_____, and all shall be _____ who are _____ against Him. In the LORD _____ the _____
  (13 Down)       (41 Across)   (28 Down)         (30 Across)  (47 Across)

of _____ _____ be justified, and shall _____.'"
  (57 Across) (54 Across)       (51 Down)

*F*ind the common "thread" that binds these two hearts together "as one in Christian love."

Start

End

*S*olve the message below to discover four major commands given by Jesus, each with a promise.

### *Clue:* MESSIAH *is* SBVVRMQ

DXAPB   TUW'   MTA   YUX

VQMFF   TUW   NB   DXAPBA.

OUTABST   TUW'   MTA   YUX

VQMFF   TUW   NB   OUTABSTBA.

CUIPRJB'   MTA   YUX   KRFF

NB   CUIPRJBT   PRJB'   MTA

RW   KRFF   NB   PRJBT   WU   YUX:

PUUA   SBMVXIB'   GIBVVBA

AUKT'   VQMEBT   WUPBWQBI'

MTA   IXTTRTP   UJBI   KRFF

NB   GXW   RTWU   YUXI   NUVUS.

"Through the LORD's mercies we are not consumed, because His compassions fail not. They are new every morning" (Lamentations 3:22–23). Great is His faithfulness . . . and His mercy.

## Across

4 Paul calls showing mercy a "present" (Romans 12:6–8)

6 Would Joseph show mercy and release this brother? (Genesis 42:24; 43:14)

7 The blind man wouldn't be "silent"—he asked Jesus for mercy (Luke 18:39)

9 "Sow . . . righteousness, 'gather up' in mercy," said Hosea (Hosea 10:12)

10 The mercies given this favorite king were Israel's for the asking (Isaiah 55:3)

12 We obtain mercy at the "seat" of grace (Hebrews 4:16)

13 As the "ordained" of God, put on tender mercies (Colossians 3:12)

15 David knew God's mercies exceeded those of this "person" (2 Samuel 24:14)

16 He and Jeduthun were chosen to thank the Lord for His enduring mercy (1 Chronicles 16:41)

17 God withheld mercy from Jerusalem and Judah for _____ years in Zechariah's time (Zechariah 1:12)

19 Jesus was made like us so He could be merciful and "devoted" High Priest (Hebrews 2:17)

23 The weightier matters of the law, Jesus said, are _____, mercy, and faith (Matthew 23:23)

24 God sends storms for correction, for the "earth," or for mercy (Job 37:13)

26 God wouldn't take His mercy from Solomon as He took it from this king (2 Samuel 7:15)

27 His descendants don't beg bread; He is merciful and "loans" (Psalm 37:25–26)

28 The mercy seat was made of this pure element (Exodus 25:17)

29 Not she, but_____

30 These "lookouts" from the house of Joseph showed mercy to a man of Bethel, but not to the rest of the city (Judges 1:22–24)

31 God extended mercy to Ezra before this king of #22 Down (Ezra 7:21–28)

32 Ben-Hadad hoped this king of Israel was as merciful as advertised (1 Kings 20:13, 31–32)

33 Their mercy saved Lot's life (Genesis 19:15–19)

## Down

1 Show no mercy to these Canaanite peoples or to the other six nations, God told Israel (Deuteronomy 7:1–2)

2 Remember Your "gentle" mercies and lovingkindness, David said (Psalm 25:6)

3 "Dear ones," said Jude, look for the mercy of our Lord (Jude 20–21)

5 Mary said, "His mercy is on those who 'stand in awe of' Him" (Luke 1:50)

8 God is kind and merciful to the "ungrateful"(Luke 6:35)

9 Her appearance at the well proved God's mercy to Abraham (Genesis 24:15–27)

11 "Mercy and truth be with you," David told _____ the Gittite, urging him to go home (2 Samuel 15:19–20)

14 God shows mercy to how many who love Him and keep His commandments? (Exodus 20:6)

15 First-person singular possessive

18 God can use "containers" of mercy to show the riches of His glory (Romans 9:23)

20 By the mercies of God, present these as a living sacrifice (Romans 12:1)

21 God will arise and have mercy on this "city," whose name means "fortification" (Psalm 102:13)

22 Thanks to mercy in the eyes of the kings of this nation, Ezra and the people could rebuild the temple (Ezra 9:9)

23 God's mercy gave him favor in the prison keeper's sight (Genesis 39:21)

25 Backsliding Israel could return and enjoy God's mercy and avoid the fall of His "wrath" (Jeremiah 3:12)

29 Be merciful, Lord, "restore" my soul, for I've sinned, said David (Psalm 41:4)

*A*ll the clues from the number puzzles below are from New Testament verses telling about the spread of the gospel and the growth of Christianity. Complete the math problems to find the numbers of the chapter and verse in the book of Revelation where John tells us how many people he saw praising God before the Lamb's throne in heaven. Then complete the following puzzle to find out what these people were saying.

**I.**

The number of people on the ship
that wrecked on the isle of Malta
(Acts 27:37)                                               = ____

Minus . . .
The number of stripes Paul
received each time he was beaten
(2 Corinthians 11:24)                                  − ____

Divided by . . .
The number times Paul was
shipwrecked (2 Corinthians 11:25)        ÷ ____

Multiplied by . . .
The number of times Paul was
beaten by Jewish persecutors (2
Corinthians 11:24)                                  × ____

Plus . . .
The number of disciples in
Jerusalem (Acts 1:15)                              + ____

Minus . . .
The approximate number of
persons who saw Jesus after the
resurrection (1 Corinthians 15:6)           − ____

Minus . . .
The number of years Aeneas was
paralyzed before he was healed
(Acts 9:33)                                              − ____

Equals . . .
The chapter number in the book of
Revelation where John saw the
saints praising God in heaven               = ____

**II.**

The number of men who believed
when Peter preached in Jerusalem
(Acts 2:41)                                              = ____

Plus . . .
The number of persons who
followed the false leader Theudas
(Acts 5:36)                                              + ____

Divided by . . .
More than this number of
conspirators sought to take Paul's
life (Acts 23:12–13)                                  ÷ ____

Multiplied by . . .
The number of Sabbaths Paul
taught in the synagogue in
Thessalonica (Acts 17:1–2)                   × ____

Plus . . .
The number of horsemen
accompanying Paul to Caesarea to
appear before Governor Felix
(Acts 23:23)                                            + ____

Divided by . . .
The number of days it took for
Paul to sail from Philippi to Troas
(Acts 20:6)                                              ÷ ____

Minus . . .
The number of years Paul stayed
in Ephesus preaching the gospel
(Acts 19:10)                                            − ____

Divided by . . .
The number of deacons appointed
to distribute provisions to the
Greek widows in Jerusalem (Acts
6:3)                                                         ÷ ____

Equals . . .
The verse number in the book of
Revelation where John saw the
saints praising God in heaven             = ____

**Answer: Revelation ____:____**

*D*ecode this message to discover one of the most wonderful passages about redemption in the Bible.

### *Clue:* MESSIAH *is* TPWWRND

R   YRFF   QRKP   ZUX   N

GPY   DPNIJ   NGB   HXJ   N

GPY   WHRIRJ   YRJDRG

ZUX'   R   YRFF   JNSP   JDP

DPNIJ   UC   WJUGP   UXJ

UC   ZUXI   CFPWD   NGB

QRKP   ZUX   N   DPNIJ   UC

CFPWD.   R   YRFF   HXJ   TZ

WHRIRJ   YRJDRG   ZUX

NGB   ONXWP   ZUX   JU

YNFS   RG   TZ   WJNJXJPW'

NGB   ZUX   YRFF   SPPH

TZ   EXBQTPGJW   NGB   BU

JDPT.

*F*irst Chronicles 29:10–15 is a great praise song by King David. Fill in the blanks from this scripture and you'll have all the words you need to complete the crossword grid! (A Word Pool is supplied to help you.)

_____ _____You,_____ _____ _____
(28 Down) (47 Down)    (64 Down) (62 Across) (7 Across)

_____ , our _____ , _____ and _____ .
(10 Down)    (2 Across) (67 Across)    (68 Across)

_____ , O Lᴏʀᴅ, is _____ _____ , the _____
(22 Across)        (15 Across) (43 Across)    (17 Across)

and the _____ , the _____ and the _____ ;
      (20 Across)    (5 Down)    (25 Down)

for all that is in _____ and in _____ _____
            (26 Across)      (33 Down) (24 Across)

Yours; _____ is the _____ , O _____ , and
    (18 Across)    (44 Across)    (35 Across)

You are _____ as _____ _____ all.
    (31 Across)    (42 Down) (63 Down)

_____ _____ and _____ come _____
(40 Across) (11 Across)    (53 Down)    (27 Across)

You, and You _____ _____ _____ (2 words).
        (4 Down)    (59 Across)

_____ _____ hand is _____ and _____ ;
(24 Down) (70 Across)    (57 Down)    (29 Down)

_____ Your _____ it is to _____ _____
(36 Across)    (38 Down)      (45 Down) (19 Down)

and to _____ _____ to all.
    (37 Across) (41 Across)

Now therefore, our God, _____ thank You and
            (56 Across)

_____ Your _____ name.
(30 Down)    (1 Down)

But _____ _____I, _____ who _____
    (52 Across) (60 Down) (58 Across)    (66 Across)

_____ people, that we _____ _____ _____
(25 Across)            (46 Down) (6 Down)  (55 Down)

to _____ _____ _____ _____ this?
    (50 Down)  (49 Down) (34 Down) (48 Across)

_____ _____ things _____ from You,
(27 Down) (9 Across)        (51 Across)

and _____ Your _____ we _____ given You.
    (65 Down)    (21 Down)    (61 Down

For we _____ _____ and _____ _____
    (14 Across) (3 Down)    (13 Across) (69 Across)

You, as _____ all _____ _____ ; our _____
    (56 Down)    (23 Down)  (8 Down)    (54 Across)

_____ _____ are _____ a _____ , and
(16 Across)(39 Across)    (32 Down) (49 Across)

without _____ .
    (12 Down)

## Word Pool

ABLE ALIENS ALL AM AND ARE ARE ARE AS AS BE BEFORE
BLESSED BOTH COME DAYS EARTH EARTH EVER EXALTED FATHER
FATHERS FOR FOREVER FROM FROM GIVE GLORIOUS GLORY
GOD GREAT GREATNESS HAND HAVE HEAD HEAVEN
HONOR HOPE IN IN IS ISRAEL KINGDOM LORD LORD MAJESTY
MAKE MIGHT MY OF OFFER ON OUR OVER OVER ALL OWN
PILGRIMS POWER POWER PRAISE REIGN RICHES SHADOW SHOULD
SO STRENGTH THE VICTORY WE WERE WHO WILLINGLY YOUR
YOURS YOURS

*(Duplicate words are intentional.)*

*In* Revelation (see puzzle 68), John recorded his vision of heaven in which he saw the redeemed "of all nations, tribes, peoples, and tongues, standing before the throne and before the Lamb, clothed with white robes, with palm branches in their hands, and crying out with a loud voice." Fit each block of squares correctly into the blank grid to reveal the message of praise to God.

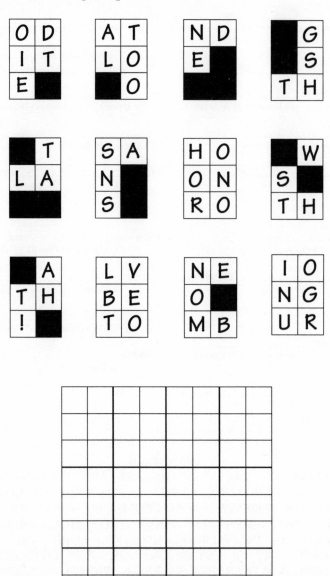

For centuries, Christians have used bells as a part of ceremonies and holidays and to call believers to church services. Find your way through this maze of bells.

Start

End

The book of James asks lots of questions! Complete the questions below, and then use the words to fill in the crossword.

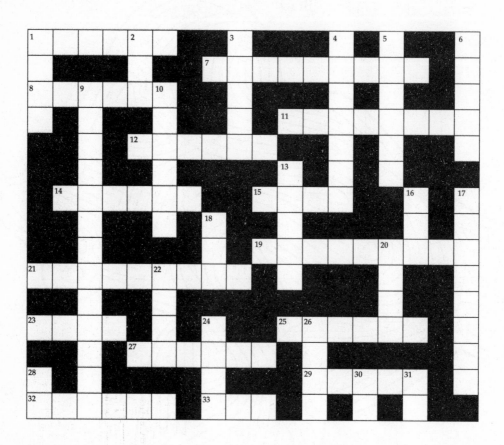

**Word Pool**

BODY BRETHREN CHEERFUL COURTS DEAD ENMITY FAITH FIGHTS FIGS GRAPEVINE HE IF IS JUDGE JUSTIFIED LIFE MAN NOBLE NOT OFFERED OLIVES PEACE PROFIT SCRIPTURE SICK SISTER SON SPIRIT SPRING TREE UNDERSTANDING VAIN YEARNS YOU

1. Does a _____ send forth fresh water
      (1 Across)
   and bitter from the same opening? (3:11)

2. Can a fig _____, my brethren,
      (20 Down)
   bear_____, or a _____ bear
   (25 Across)      (21 Across)
   _____? (3:12)
   (24 Down)

3. Who is wise and _____ among you? (3:13)
            (9 Down)

4. Where do wars and _____ come from
            (32 Across)
   among you? (4:1)

5. Who are you to _____ another? (4:12)
            (3 Down)

6. What is your _____ ? (4:14)
         (26 Down)

7. _____ anyone among you
   (30 Down)
   suffering? (5:13)

8. Is anyone _____ ? (5:13)
      (11 Across)

9. Is anyone among you _____ ? (5:14)
               (1 Down)

10. Do not the rich oppress you and drag you

    into the _____ ? (2:6)
      (8 Across)

11. Do they not blaspheme that _____ name
                  (6 Down)
    by which you are called? (2:7)

12. What does it _____, my _____, if
         (14 Across)      (17 Down)
    someone says _____ has faith but does
            (31 Down)
    not have works? (2:14)

13. _____ a brother or _____ is naked
    (28 Down)            (12 Across)
    and destitute of daily food, and one of you

    says to them,"Depart in _____ , be
                  (13 Down)
    warmed and filled," but you do not give

    them the things which are needed for the

    _____ , what does it profit? (2:15–16)
    (23 Across)

14. Do you _____ know that friendship
         (2 Down)
    with the world is _____ with God? (4:4)
               (27 Across)

15. Do _____ think that the _____
      (16 Down)            (19 Across)
    says in _____,"The _____ who
         (22 Down)      (10 Down)
    dwells in us _____ jealously"? (4:5)
            (5 Down)

16. But do you want to know, O foolish

    _____, that faith without works is
    (18 Down)
    _____? Was not Abraham our father
    (15 Across)
    _____ by works when he _____
    (7 Across)                  (4 Down)
    Isaac his _____on the altar? Do you see
            (33 Across)
    that faith was working together with his

    works, and by works _____ was made
                  (29 Across)
    perfect? (2:20–22)

*D*ecode the following message to discover a Bible truth about the power of our words.

*Clue:* MESSIAH *is* GOAAKSL

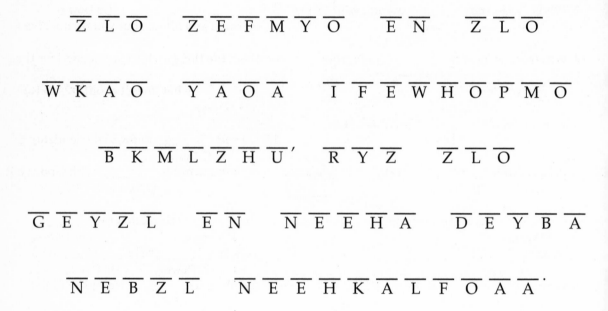

Z L O   Z E F M Y O   E N   Z L O

W K A O   Y A O A   I F E W H O P M O

B K M L Z H U'   R Y Z   Z L O

G E Y Z L   E N   N E E H A   D E Y B A

N E B Z L   N E E H K A L F O A A.

*S*tring together the letters below to reveal a Bible verse about the watchfulness of our heavenly Father.

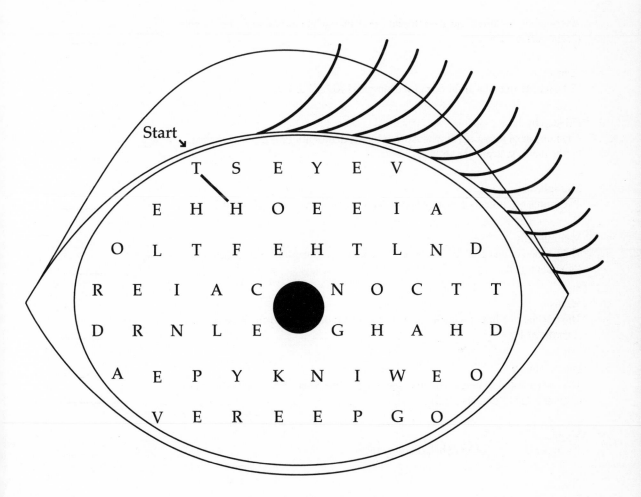

Start

| T | S | E | Y | E | V |
| --- | --- | --- | --- | --- | --- |

| E | H | H | O | E | E | I | A |
| --- | --- | --- | --- | --- | --- | --- | --- |

| O | L | T | F | E | H | T | L | N | D |

| R | E | I | A | C | N | O | C | T | T |

| D | R | N | L | E | G | H | A | H | D |

| A | E | P | Y | K | N | I | W | E | O |

| V | E | R | E | E | P | G | O |

When Jesus turned the water into wine He made enough so the wedding host wouldn't run out again. Complete the puzzle below to find out how much water miraculously became wine.

The number of baths of oil given to the woodsmen who cut timber for the temple (2 Chronicles 2:10) $=$ \_\_\_\_\_

Minus . . .
The capacity in baths of the Sea of the temple (1 Kings 7:26) $-$ \_\_\_\_\_

Divided by . . .
The number of measures of wheat owed by the debtor after his bill was reduced by the unjust steward (Luke 16:7) $\div$ \_\_\_\_\_

Multiplied by . . .
The number of homers of barley Hosea paid to get Gomer back (Hosea 3:2) $\times$ \_\_\_\_\_

Multiplied by . . .
The fraction of an ephah of fine flour offered with a young bull as a sacriftce (Numbers 15:9) $\times$ \_\_\_\_\_

Minus . . .
The fraction of a hin of wine that was to be offered daily as a drink offering (Exodus 29:40) $-$ \_\_\_\_\_

Divided by . . .
The least amount of homers of quail gathered in the desert when God sent flocks of quail to eat (Numbers 11:32) $\div$ \_\_\_\_\_

Minus . . .
The omer is \_\_\_\_\_ of an ephah (Exodus 16:36) $-$ \_\_\_\_\_

Plus . . .
The number of omers of manna gathered for each person on the sixth day of the week (Exodus 16:22) $+$ \_\_\_\_\_

Divided by . . .
The number of seahs of barley sold for a shekel during the famine in Samaria (2 Kings 7:1) $\div$ \_\_\_\_\_

Equals . . .
The number of waterpots filled with water that Jesus turned into wine (John 2:6) $=$ \_\_\_\_\_

$W$hat kind of wisdom do we need in this life? The kind that leads us to build our lives upon the Rock.

## Across

2 "Joyful" is he who finds wisdom (Proverbs 3:13)

6 Jesus increased in wisdom and _____ (Luke 2:52)

8 Wisdom is better than these red jewels (Proverbs 8:11)

11 The mouth of the "godly" speaks wisdom (Proverbs 10:31)

13 "To _____ or not . . ."

14 Wisdom from above is "undefiled" (James 3:17)

15 He rewarded Joseph's wisdom (Genesis 41:39–40)

16 The beginning of wisdom (4 words) (Proverbs 9:10)

18 Not off, but _____

20 He learned the wisdom of the Egyptians (Acts 7:22)

23 Who put wisdom in the "brain"? (Job 38:36)

24 Wisdom is the "primary" thing (Proverbs 4:7)

25 A wise man fears "wickedness" (Proverbs 14:16)

26 A wise man shouldn't "delight" in his wisdom (Jeremiah 9:23)

27 Wisdom and "strength" are God's (Daniel 2:20)

## Down

1 Wisdom is better than weapons of "combat" (Ecclesiastes 9:18)

3 The wisdom of wise men shall "crumble" (Isaiah 29:14)

4 Wise-hearted women spun "thread" of goats' hair (Exodus 35:26)

5 Paul: A "man who owed" to the wise and unwise (Romans 1:14)

7 Huram from _____ had wisdom in bronze work (1 Kings 7:13–14)

9 God's testimony makes the "ingenuous" wise (Psalm 19:7)

10 "Divide the living child in two!" he said (1 Kings 3:15, 25)

12 By wisdom, God made the "skies" (Psalm 136:5)

13 This wise son of Uri did artwork (Exodus 31:2–4)

14 Put faith in God's "force," not human wisdom (1 Corinthians 2:5)

16 God uses the _____ to shame the wise (1 Corinthians 1:27)

17 The depth of the "wealth" of God's wisdom (Romans 11:33)

19 The thoughts of the wise are "useless" (1 Corinthians 3:20)

21 Wisdom makes the face "glow" (Ecclesiastes 8:1)

22 Don't be unwise; understand God's "intention" (Ephesians 5:17)

23 The three wise men

One of the items in each set below doesn't belong to the set. Cross out the one that doesn't belong and identify the reason why.

1. Moses, Elijah, Jesus, John the Baptist

2. Coin, Mustard seed, Son, Sheep

3. Burning bush, Shadrach, Tares, Faith

4. Rahab, Gomer, Mary Magdalene, Zacchaeus

5. Upper Room, Heart, Tabernacle, Zion

6. Sarah, Jochebed, Hannah, Elizabeth

7. Hebrews, Romans, Galatians, Philemon

8. Levi, Issachar, Dan, Joel

9. Jehoshaphat, Jehoiakim, Josiah, Jotham

10. Matthew, Mark, Luke, John

11. Faith, Joy, Hope, Love

12. Athens, Corinth, Galatia, Thessalonica

13. Apostles, Scribes, Prophets, Teachers

14. Zacharias, Philip, Titus, Herod

15. Gentleness, Freedom, Self-control, Peace

16. Ram's horn, Manna, Aaron's rod that budded, Stone tablets

17. Urim and thummin, Rainbow, Fleece, Pillar of cloud

18. James, John the Baptist, Stephen, Timothy

19. Cattle, Fish, Man, Serpent

20. Lamp, Fire, Chariot, Sword

# Letter to Rome

When Paul wrote his letter to the church at Rome, there was no postal service to deliver it for him. It had to be hand-carried.

Since the Jews were plotting against Paul, he had to make a detour on his way to Rome. He asked Phoebe, a friend and a "servant of the church" in Cenchrea (near Corinth), to take the letter to the Roman believers.

Phoebe must visit twelve of Paul's friends before she delivers his letter to Rome. Do not cross back over a path that you have already used.

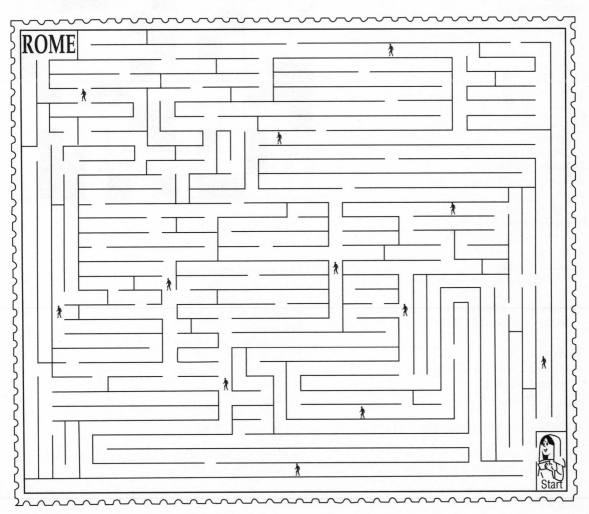

*M*any of the answers come from the life of Samuel and those associated with him. When you complete the crossword, assemble and rearrange the circled letters to reveal a hidden message about Samuel.

## Across

1 Samuel anointed Saul, who was the ____ ____ of Israel (2 words)
7 God to Moses: "Tell them I ____ has sent you" (Exodus 3:14)
9 Exclamation
10 Lassie's breed
12 Victory
15 ____ wife turned out to be pretty salty, (poss.)
16 Samuel's mom (1 Samuel 1:20)
17 Do re ____
18 Initials on the side of a ship
20 Priest, young Samuel's boss (1 Samuel 1:25)
21 Tear
22 Diminish
25 Lease
27 Market
28 Barley and oats
31 David's instrument
32 Felonious fire
34 Officer in training
35 David's father (1 Samuel 17:17)
37 1992 riot scene (abbr.)
38 Water transportation
39 Either's partner
40 What Saul was looking for when he met Samuel (1 Samuel 9:3)
41 Having it in a city resulted in a plague of tumors (1 Samuel 5:6–12)

## Down

1 Elkanah's relationship to Samuel (1 Samuel 1:19–20)
2 ____ cats and dogs
3 Avoid
4 David's daughter, pursued by Amnon (2 Samuel 13:1)
5 Duke University state (abbr.)
6 He fell for David (1 Samuel 21:9)

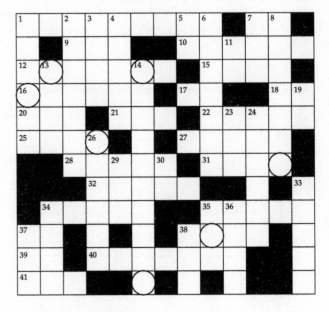

7 Hgt. for an airplane
8 Reason for a trip
11 ____ and behold!
13 Abnormal breathing noise
14 Goliath was one
19 Direction from Chicago to Miami
23 Feather or constrictor
24 Capture
26 Pro ball player's cause for a move
29 Plural of am
30 Negatory, good buddy
33 Mails
34 Singer Vicki ____
35 Grief's opposite
36 Where the star was
37 Mauna ____
38 Where Samuel was when God spoke to him as a child (1 Samuel 3:3–4)

Hidden message:

__ __ __ __ __ __ __

*J*eremiah 51:19–20 presents a description of the Lord of hosts as "my battle-ax and weapons of war." In the box of letters below, find seventeen things that will be destroyed or broken in pieces by the Lord of hosts. (See Jeremiah 51:20–23.) (Note: Two of the items have more than one word.)

```
F   A   R   M   F   L   C   O   S   R   E   L   U   R
D   R   E   H   P   E   H   S   C   K   G   O   V   E
P   E   N   S   F   M   A   S   N   O   S   E   H   R
I   H   A   H   O   I   R   E   D   I   R   H   S   N
E   S   T   E   R   E   I   A   T   I   O   P   K   O
K   N   I   P   N   V   O   N   N   R   N   H   O   R
P   I   O   H   O   R   T   G   S   K   R   N   Y   S
T   O   N   G   S   O   M   E   C   I   E   E   A   M
A   N   S   G   F   W   I   F   O   D   V   R   D   Y
F   O   E   M   D   A   N   L   I   S   O   F   O   O
Y   L   R   L   R   O   A   A   N   O   G   K   L   U
I   N   O   M   A   I   M   T   M   I   E   D   O   N
K   G   T   C   V   D   E   S   A   O   O   G   C   G
E   D   O   I   K   N   K   N   F   M   W   N   I   K
V   N   A   M   G   N   U   O   Y   S   H   E   P   H
G   O   I   T   A   N   X   F   L   W   Y   N   E   E
O   F   A   R   M   E   R   N   O   A   O   I   D   R
R   O   N   R   N   V   E   A   M   M   K   A   M   D
```

*H*is people might stray, but God always has a plan for bringing them back into the fold. This puzzle is taken from Jeremiah 31 and concerns Israel's restoration.

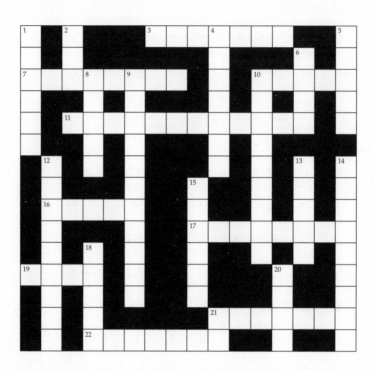

## Across

3 Crying (v. 9)
7 God "bought back" Jacob (v. 11)
10 The seed of Israel could "end" (v. 36)
11 God's "night lights" (3 words) (v. 35)
16 Surveyor's line will go over this hill (v. 39)
17 God's "agreement" with Israel (v. 31)
19 The fathers ate ____ grapes (v. 29)
21 The "remaining part" of Israel (v. 7)
22 Watchmen will cry on Mount ____ (v. 6)

## Down

1 Valley and fields won't be "tossed" down again (v. 40)
2 God will forget their "wrongdoing" (v. 34)
4 Their soul will have abundance (v. 14)
5 Grain (v. 12)
6 God put his "statutes" (pl.) in their minds (v. 33)
8 They survived the "saber" (v. 2)
9 God will sow the houses of Israel and Judah with the seed of ____ ____ ____ (3 words) (v. 27)
10 Scolded (v. 18)
12 Set up "markers" (v. 21)
13 "A voice was heard in ____" (v. 15)
14 Imprisonment (v. 23)
15 She cries for her children (v. 15)
18 After #8 Down, they found this in the wilderness (v. 2)
20 They'll plant these (sing.) on mountains (v. 5)
21 Room (abbr.)

# Keys to the Kingdom

*J*esus asked His disciples, "Who do men say that I, the Son of Man, am?" and then again, "Who do you say that I am?" (Matthew 16:13, 15). Peter replied to the question, "You are the Christ, the Son of the living God" (v. 16). Jesus then said to Peter, "Blessed are you, Simon Bar-Jonah, for flesh and blood has not revealed this to you, but My Father who is in heaven. And I also say to you that you are Peter, and on this rock I will build My church, and the gates of Hades shall not prevail against it. And I will give you the keys of the kingdom of heaven, and whatever you bind on earth will be bound in heaven, and whatever you loose on earth will be loosed in heaven" (v. 17–19).

St. Peter's Cross usually depicts these keys of the kingdom with an inverted cross—the shape of the cross on which Peter was martyred. One key is usually shown in silver, the other in gold.

Start

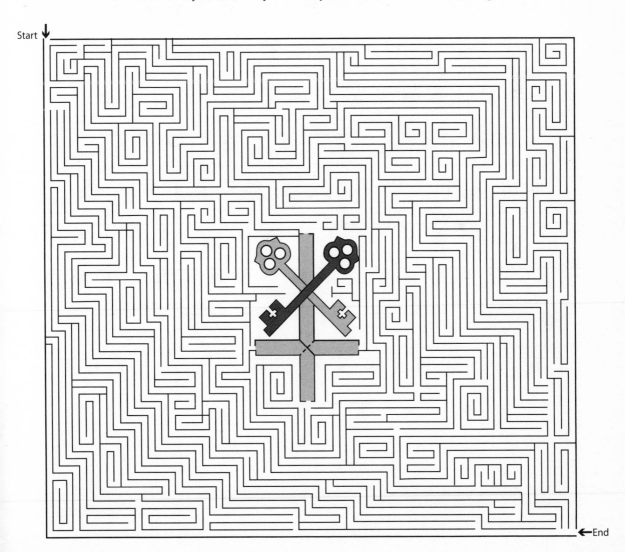

←End

Solve the puzzle below to find one of the passages in the Psalms that speaks of the Messiah.

## Clue: MESSIAH *is* GKDDIMQ

I̲  B̲I̲S̲S̲  U̲V̲M̲I̲D̲K̲  A̲F̲C̲'

P̲F̲V̲  A̲F̲C̲  Q̲M̲X̲K̲  M̲T̲D̲B̲K̲V̲K̲O̲

G̲K̲'  M̲T̲O̲  Q̲M̲X̲K̲  N̲K̲L̲F̲G̲K̲

G̲A̲  D̲M̲S̲X̲M̲W̲I̲F̲T̲  W̲Q̲K̲.

D̲W̲F̲T̲K̲  B̲Q̲I̲L̲Q̲  W̲Q̲K̲

N̲C̲I̲S̲O̲K̲V̲D̲  V̲K̲R̲K̲L̲W̲K̲O̲

Q̲M̲D̲  N̲K̲L̲F̲G̲K̲  W̲Q̲K̲  L̲Q̲I̲K̲P̲

L̲F̲V̲T̲K̲V̲D̲W̲F̲T̲K̲.  W̲Q̲I̲D̲  B̲M̲D̲

W̲Q̲K̲  S̲F̲V̲O̲D̲'  O̲F̲I̲T̲J̲';  I̲W̲

I̲D̲  G̲M̲V̲X̲K̲S̲F̲C̲D̲  I̲T̲  F̲C̲V̲

K̲A̲K̲D̲.

*T*his crossword will sweep out the cobwebs of your mind and refresh your attitude! And when you're finished, there is a special message for you in the circled letters reading diagonally down.

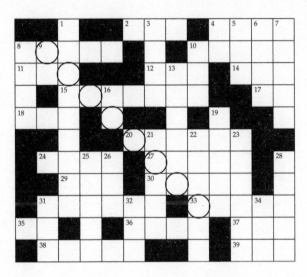

## Across

2 Cleopatra's snake
4 Jump
8 Scrub
10 Wash
11 Buddy
12 Name for a lion
14 What #12 Across is
15 Biblical healings often involved this disease
17 "Rise and ____ healed!"
18 Place to take a bath
20 He was made clean in the Jordan River (2 Kings 5:1–14)
24 "You are already clean because of the ____ which I have spoken to you." (John 15:3)
27 Boulder
29 Largest number of lepers that Jesus healed at one time recorded in the Bible (Luke 17:14–17)
30 Red dye
31 Bind up wheat
33 Game with a bull's-eye
35 International press organization (abbr.)
36 ¿Como ____ usted?
37 Hawaiian greeting piece
38 Resource, benefit
39 Affirmative

## Down

1 Mid-highway fee collection point (2 words)
3 Farm structure
4 Fa sol ____
5 I.e. and et al's cousin
6 Evil king of Israel; Elijah's foe (1 Kings 16:30)
7 He had a rooftop vision about clean things (Acts 10:9–15)
8 Stain
9 L.A.'s state (abbr.)
10 Young man
13 Manor
16 Philadelphia's home (abbr.)
19 Desert grub for children of Israel
21 Priestly substance of ritual cleansing (Hebrews 9:13–15)
22 Sunday follower
23 Almost
25 Bulrushes
26 Genetic factor
28 Desert watering hole
31 Rest and rejuvenation place
32 Short for retired soldier
34 Place to set your golf ball

# PUZZLE ANSWERS

**1**

**3**

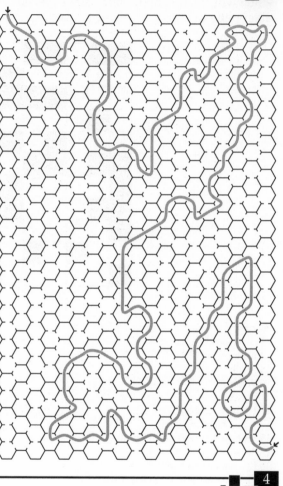

**2**

**4**

RU**T**H
JEHOS**H**ABEATH
JA**E**L
**E**LIZABETH
T**A**MAR
NAO**M**I
RE**B**EKAH
**S**ARAH
A**B**IGAIL
DEBO**R**AH
ZI**P**PORAH
JOCHEBE**D**
AS**E**NATH

**THE LAMB'S BRIDE**

**5**

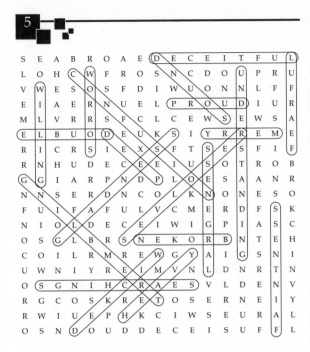

**7**

**6**

He shall be like a tree planted by the rivers of water, that brings forth its fruit in its season, whose leaf also shall not wither; and whatever he does shall prosper. (Psalm 1:3)

# PUZZLE ANSWERS

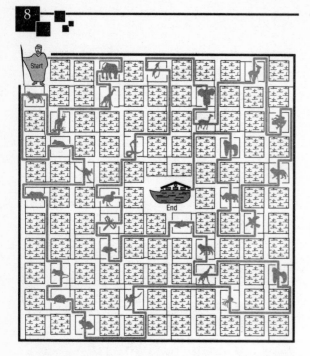

Watch, stand fast in the faith, be brave, be strong. Let all that you do be done with love. (1 Corinthians 16:13–14)

HEA**R**TS
**F**EAST
**J**OY
S**O**NG
GOOD TH**I**NG
DAN**C**E
FI**E**LD
AGAIN **I** WILL SAY, REJOICE!
HA**N**D
GEN**T**ILES
**H**EAVENS
NAM**E**
**L**IPS
GO**O**DNESS
DESE**R**T
WOR**D**
SAL**V**ATION
EXCEEDING**L**Y
**W**INGS
VENGE**A**NCE
**Y**OUTH
TRU**S**T

**REJOICE IN THE LORD ALWAYS**
(Philippians 4:4)

# PUZZLE ANSWERS

## 13

STRENGTH
HAIL
THUNDERBOLT
TIME
FOUNDATIONS
JOY
SEA
MORNING STARS
DEATH
TERRITORY
SNOW
FOOD
WATER
BREADTH
ICE
DAWN
LOOSE
WISDOM
WIND
LIGHT
LIGHTNINGS
UNDERSTANDING
WAY
SPRINGS
FROST
DEW

**THE MAJESTY OF THE ALMIGHTY GOD**

## 15

## 14

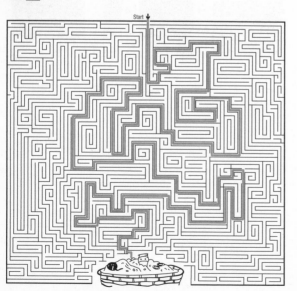

## 16

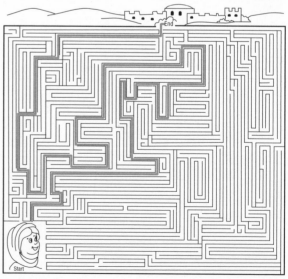

17

5,000 − 4,000 ÷ 5 × 3 − (70 × 7) or 490
− 70 × 11 − 40 ÷ 100 × 10 − 1 + 38 + 3
− 12 − 30 − 18 − 8 ÷ 12 = 1
I and My Father are one. (John 10:30)

18

19

20

My food is to do the will of Him who
sent Me, and to finish His work. (John
4:34)

# PUZZLE ANSWERS

## 21

BO**D**Y
SH**O**WBREAD
EA**T**
FAT**H**ER
AB**I**DES
FLE**S**H
DR**I**NK
LIVI**N**G
ETE**R**NAL LIFE
UPP**E**R ROOM
EXA**M**INE
NEW COV**E**NANT
COM**M**UNION
**B**LOOD
FO**R**EVER
UNLE**A**VENED
HU**N**GER
PRO**C**LAIM
GAV**E** THANKS
PASS**O**VER
LI**F**E
RE**M**ISSION
B**R**EAD

**DO THIS IN REMEMBRANCE OF ME**
(Luke 22:19)

Heaven and earth will pass away, but My words will by no means pass away. But of that day and hour no one knows, not even the angels in heaven, nor the Son, but only the Father.
(Mark 13:31–32)

## 24

**25**

About opposite "the fourth watch of the night"
And before "night"
And even before "evening"
After "dawn"
And after "early in the morning"
Before "the tenth hour"
And after "the third hour" of His crucifixion
Ended at the "ninth hour" when Jesus cried from the cross.
Began at "the sixth hour" when Jesus sat by the well at Sychar

The time period is the "sixth to ninth hours" (about 12 noon to 3 P.M.).

"Now when the sixth hour had come, there was darkness over the whole land until the ninth hour" [as Jesus hung on the cross]. (Mark 15:33)

**26**

**27**

**28**

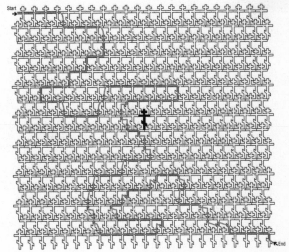

**29**

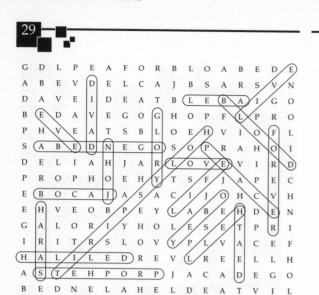

```
G D L P E A F O R B L O A B E D E
A B E V D E L C A J B S A R S V N
D A V E I D E A T B L E B A I G O
B E D A V E G O G H O P F L P R O
P H V E A T S B L O E H V I O F L
S A B E D N E G O S O P R A H O I
D E L I A H J A R L O V E V I R D
P R O P H O E H Y T S F J A P E C
E B O C A J A S A C I J O H C V H
E H V E O B P E Y L A B E H D E N
G A L O R I Y H O L E S E T P R I
I R I T R S L O V Y P L V A C E F
H A L I L E D R E V L R E E L L H
A S T E H P O R P J A C A D E G O
B E D N E L A H E L D E A T V I L
E V H N S E R A H E L B D A L L G
```

OBEY  EVE  JOHN  PROPHETS  LIFE  SARAH
ABEL  DAVID  LOVE  HOLY SPIRIT  GLORY
ABED-NEGO  DELILAH  JACOB  HELL
DEATH PEACE  FOREVER  BLOOD  EVIL

**31**

ISAAC            AZARIAH
JEHU             PETHUEL
NOAH             ELEAZAR
SOLOMON          JACOB
JEHOSHAPHAT      JESSE
AMRAM

### Unscrambled letters:
### INHERITANCE

**30**

**R**EST
**E**DIFIED
**M**OTHER'S
**E**NEMIES
**M**ATTER
**B**RETHREN
**E**NTER
**R**ESTING
**T**RIBULATION
**H**OLY
**E**NJOY
**S**EVENTH
**A**SLEEP
**B**ECAUSE
**B**OUNTIFULLY
**A**DVERSITY
**T**ROUBLE
**H**ALLOWED
**D**OVE
**A**RK
**Y**OKE

**REMEMBER THE SABBATH DAY**

**32**

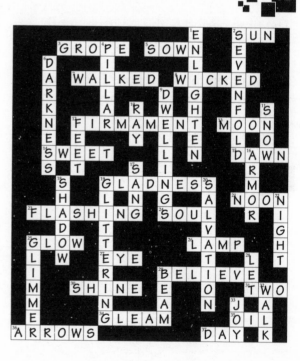

## 33

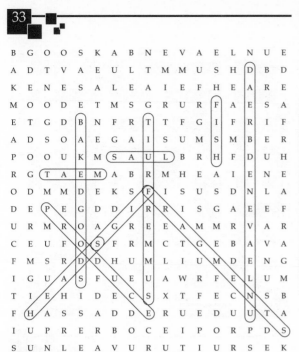

```
B G O O S K A B N E V A E L N U E
A D T V A E U L T M M U S H D B D
K E N E S A L E A I E F H E A R E
M O O D E T M S G R U R F A E S A
E T G D B N F R T T F G I F R I F
A D S O A E G A I S U M S M B E R
P O O U K M S A U L B R H F D U H
R G T A E M A B R M H E A I E N E
O D M M D E K S F I S U S D N L A
D E P E G D D I R R I S G A E E F
U R M R O A G R E E A M M R V A R
C E U F O S F R M C T G E B A V A
F M S R D D H U M L I U M D E N G
I G U A S F U E U A W R F E L U M
T I E H I D E C S X T F E C N S B
F H A S S A D D E R U E D U U T A
I U P R E R B O C E I P O R P D S
S U N L E A V U R U T I U R S E K
```

## 34

## 35

```
¹S E V E N  ³B R O T H E R⁴S  ⁵R  ⁶A L
 T          L      T     R  ⁷H E A L  ⁸B L O T ⁹S O U T  ¹⁰P A I N
 E          A      O     H   N  I   M         E          L I V E
 P          L      D     I   ¹¹P A R D O N    N          I
 H          ¹²P  ¹³A T O N E M E N T   ¹⁴C    T          ⁵R E
 E          A      I       B  H                          M I
 N          ¹⁵T R E S P A S S E S  B E L I E V E S       S S
            ¹⁶I D O L S  ¹⁷D  ¹⁸D E E D S  ¹⁹P            I O
             V        E     E     E        H            O N
            ²⁰F R A G R A N T O I L  L     A            ²¹W A L K
             N        R     B  ²²R  O      R            O
            ²³R E A D Y      I     O  V    ²⁴N I N E V E H
```

**Bonus: REPENTANCE**

## 36

Do not fear, little flock, for it is your Father's good pleasure to give you the kingdom. (Luke 12:32)

## 37

```
              ¹D    ²S    ³J         ⁴L
⁵G R A V E S   H         A    ⁶P      I
               ⁷P E A C E   O   E      V
               H           B   ⁸H O P E
⁹N  ¹⁰J O S E P H  E  R   P    P
A   U         T       D   L
T   D         A       ¹¹D W E L L
¹²K I N G     B       E   F
O   G         L   ¹³S  E
¹⁴R  N  E V E R L A S T I N G
A             A   I   L   ¹⁷V
T             ¹⁸B   N   E   A
¹⁹D  ²⁰P R I N C E W  ²¹H  L
²²C L E A N S E      W   O  L
I  V         A       ²³S T A T U T E Y
N  I  ²⁴S T I C K    S
G  D         H
```

**38**

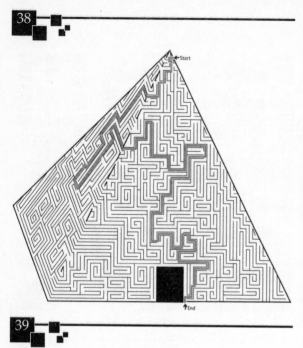

Start → / End ↑

**39**

CA**TT**LE
**H**EAD
STOR**E**HOUSES
ESTA**B**LISH
**PL**ENTY
ABOV**E**
INCREA**S**E
TREA**S**URE
FRU**I**T
COU**N**TRY
**G**O
PR**O**DUCE
**F**LOCKS
W**O**RK
**B**OWL
**HE**RDS
LAN**D**
H**I**GH
ENEMI**E**S
RAI**N**
**C**OME
L**E**ND

**THE BLESSING OF OBEDIENCE**

**40**

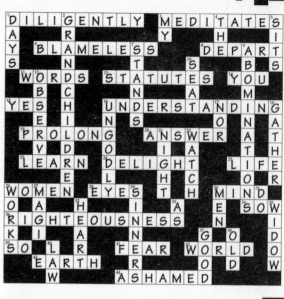

**41**

$2 \times 11 \times 6 \times 130 \times 70 \div 2 + [10 \times 5 \times 5 \times 5 \times 2 = 2{,}500] + [(12 + 12 + 12 + 12) \times 7 = 336] + [50 \times 2 = 100] + 14 = 603{,}550$

**42**

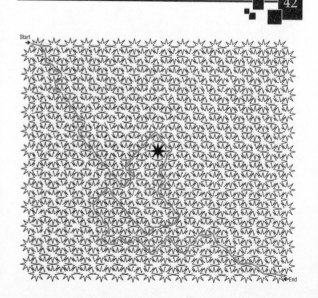

Start → ← End

**43**

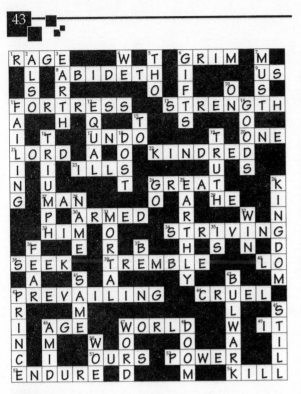

**44**

TUMORS
ITCH
MADNESS
SCORCHING
CONFUSION
DESTROYED
OPPRESSED
PERISH
BOILS
FEVER
MILDEW
BLINDNESS
DUST
SWORD
REBUKE
DEFEATED
PLUNDERED
INFLAMMATION
TROUBLESOME
CONSUMPTION
SCAB
PLAGUE

**THE CURSE OF DISOBEDIENCE**

**45**

**46**

| A | B | C | D | A | U | R | J | A | H | N | A | Z | A | R | D | E | F | O | P | Q |
|---|---|---|---|---|---|---|---|---|---|---|---|---|---|---|---|---|---|---|---|---|
| G | H | I | P | S | G | R | A | H | T | I | B | A | T | U | R | S | T | U | V | W |
| J | K | L | I | H | Z | A | A | H | A | I | B | A | T | S | J | A | I | R | S | N |
| M | N | O | A | U | T | Z | R | U | H | B | I | S | H | U | A | I | N | S | H | U |
| O | R | S | T | N | E | J | N | J | P | R | L | U | S | N | T | U | V | E | U | T |
| T | U | V | S | A | N | A | I | N | E | I | A | S | N | A | Y | C | H | U | S | Z |
| W | X | Y | H | M | A | I | S | E | R | A | Z | E | R | M | A | R | E | P | H | A |
| Z | A | B | U | M | L | R | U | S | A | L | J | J | A | Z | T | H | J | E | S | U |
| C | D | E | T | I | S | U | R | A | Z | A | L | S | I | U | L | A | Z | A | R | U |
| F | G | H | Y | T | U | S | I | A | J | I | A | N | E | S | N | A | I | T | A | B |
| I | J | K | C | E | H | S | U | H | C | Y | T | U | E | J | I | T | H | A | D | O |
| L | M | N | A | L | B | A | T | I | M | M | A | N | S | E | R | C | A | S | E | U |

**47**

Honest weights and scales are the LORD's;
all the weights in the bag are His work.
(Proverbs 16:11)

# PUZZLE ANSWERS

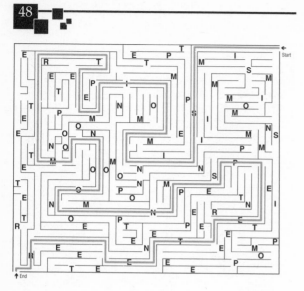

**48**

**49**

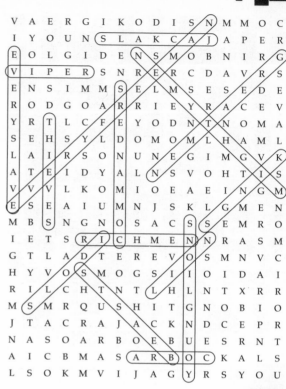

**50**

**51**

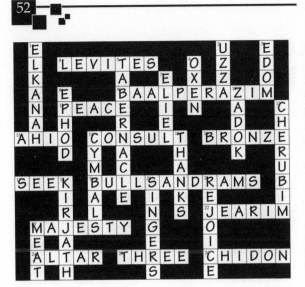

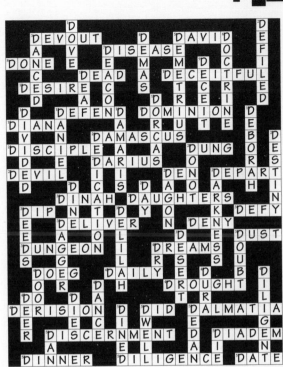

Naked I came from my mother's womb,
and naked shall I return there. The LORD
gave, and the LORD has taken away;
blessed be the name of the LORD. (Job 1:21)

# PUZZLE ANSWERS

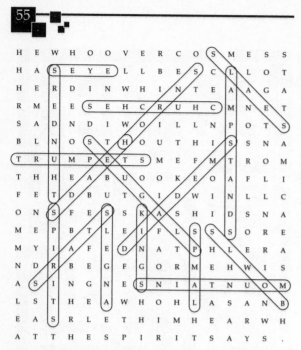

## 55

Hidden verses: He who overcomes shall be clothed in white garments, and I will not blot out his name from the Book of Life; but I will confess his name before My Father and before His angels. He who has an ear, let him hear what the Spirit says. (Revelation 3:5–6)

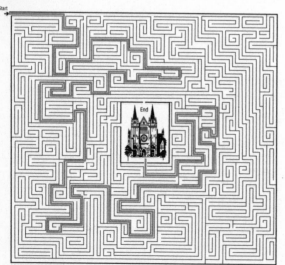

## 56

Fall on us and hide us from the face of Him who sits on the throne and from the wrath of the Lamb! For the great day of His wrath has come, and who is able to stand? (Revelation 6:16–17)

**59**

PATHS
RIGHTEOUSNESS
MAKES
WALK
SHADOW
GREEN
LEADS
WITH
RESTORES
COMFORT
MERCY
PASTURES
HOUSE
ENEMIES
PREPARE
HIS
DEATH
RUNS
DOWN
STILL
SURELY
THOUGH
NAMES
EVIL
LIE
ANOINT
ROD
STAFF
WATERS
VALLEY
GOODNESS
TABLE

**THE LORD IS MY SHEPHERD, I SHALL NOT WANT**

**60**

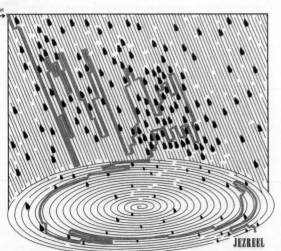

Start →

JEZREEL
End

**61**

**62**

CHRISTIAN
FAITHFUL
WORLD
ANGELS
HOLY NIGHT
THREE
MIDNIGHT
LITTLE
MANGER
BETHLEHEM
FIRST

**SILENT NIGHT, HOLY NIGHT**

# PUZZLE ANSWERS

63

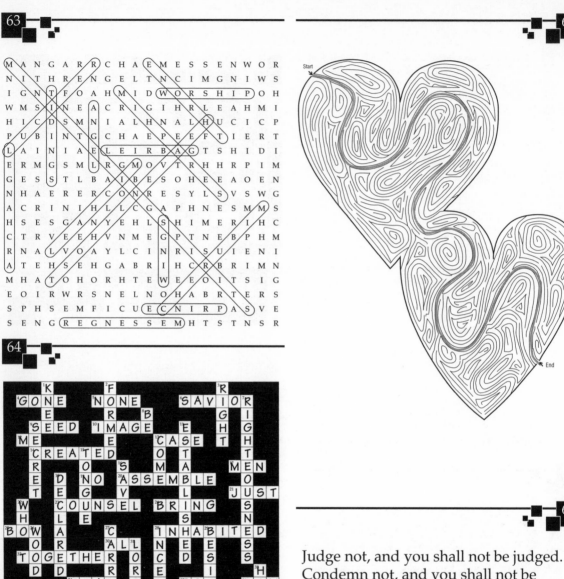

65

64

66

Judge not, and you shall not be judged. Condemn not, and you shall not be condemned. Forgive, and you will be forgiven. Give, and it will be given to you: good measure, pressed down, shaken together, and running over will be put into your bosom. (Luke 6:37–38a)

**67**

**70**

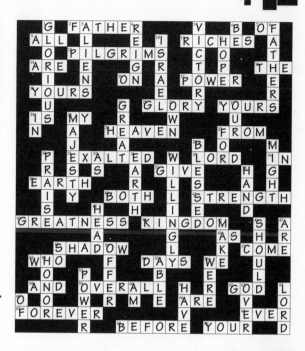

**68**

I. $276 - 39 \div 3 \times 5 + 120 - 500 - 8 = 7$

II. $3{,}000 + 400 \div 40 \times 3 + 70 \div 5 - 2 \div 7 = 9$

A great multitude which no one could number. (Revelation 7:9)

**69**

I will give you a new heart and put a new spirit within you; I will take the heart of stone out of your flesh and give you a heart of flesh. I will put My Spirit within you and cause you to walk in My statutes, and you will keep My judgments and do them. (Ezekiel 36:26–27)

**71**

| S | A | L | V | A | T | I | O |
|---|---|---|---|---|---|---|---|
| N |   | B | E | L | O | N | G |
| S |   | T | O |   | O | U | R |
|   |   | G | O | D |   | W | H | O |
|   |   | S | I | T | S |   | O | N |
| T | H | E |   | T | H | R | O |
| N | E |   | A | N | D |   | T |
| O |   | T | H | E |   | L | A |
| M | B | ! |   |   |   |   |

Salvation belongs to our God who sits on the throne, and to the Lamb! (Revelation 7:10)

# PUZZLE ANSWERS

Start

End

The tongue of the wise uses knowledge rightly, but the mouth of fools pours forth foolishness. (Proverbs 15:2)

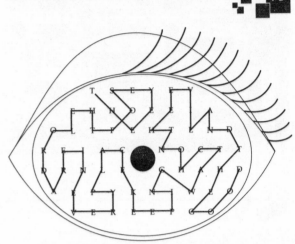

The eyes of the LORD are in every place, keeping watch on the evil and the good. (Proverbs 15:3)

$$20,000 - 2,000 \div 80 \times 1.5 \times .3 - .25 \div 10 - .1 + 2 \div 2 = 6$$

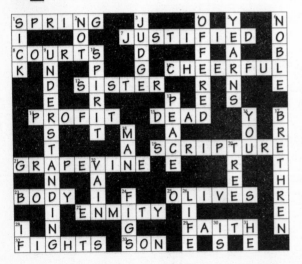

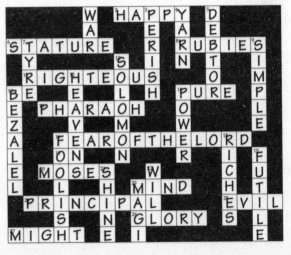

1. John the Baptist was not on the Mount of Transfiguration
2. Mustard seed was not lost and then found
3. Tares were burned up in the fire, the others were not consumed
4. Gomer was an unrepentant sinner
5. Upper Room is not described in the Bible as a place where God dwells
6. Jochebed was not a barren woman before God blessed her with children
7. Hebrews was not written by Paul
8. Joel is not the name of a tribe of Israel
9. Jehoiakim was not a good king
10. John is not a synoptic gospel
11. Joy is not one of the three virtues
12. Athens is not the location of a church that received a letter from Paul
13. Scribes is not one of the offices in the church
14. Titus was not visited by angels
15. Freedom is not one of the fruits of the Spirit in Galations 5:22–23
16. Ram's horn is not one of the items in the ark of the covenant
17. Rainbow was not a means of divine guidance in the Bible
18. Timothy was not put to death for his faith
19. Fish were not created on the sixth day
20. Chariot is not a term used to describe the Bible

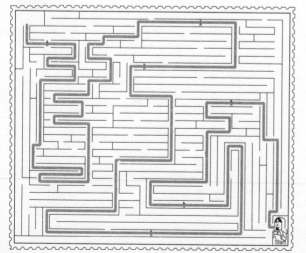

Hidden message: PROPHET

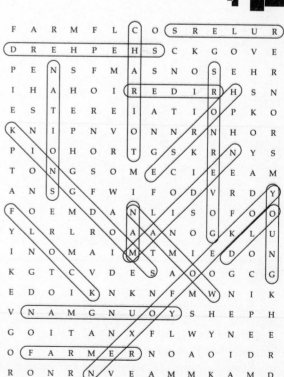

# PUZZLE ANSWERS

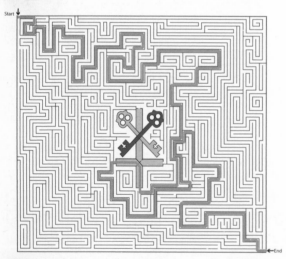

I will praise You, for You have answered me, and have become my salvation. The stone which the builders rejected has become the chief cornerstone. This was the LORD's doing; it is marvelous in our eyes. (Psalm 118:21–23)